# Katherine Paterson

# WHO WROTE THAT?

ASHLAND PUBLIC LIBRARY
66 FRONT STREET
ASHLAND, MA 01721

# Katherine Paterson

*John Bankston*

**Foreword by**
*Kyle Zimmer*

CHELSEA HOUSE
PUBLISHERS
An imprint of Infobase Publishing

**Katherine Paterson**

Copyright © 2010 by Infobase Publishing

All rights reserved. No part of this book may be reproduced or utilized in any form or by any means, electronic or mechanical, including photocopying, recording, or by any information storage or retrieval systems, without permission in writing from the publisher. For information, contact:

Chelsea House
An imprint of Infobase Publishing
132 West 31st Street
New York, NY 10001

**Library of Congress Cataloging-in-Publication Data**
Bankston, John, 1974-
  Katherine Paterson / John Bankston.
  p. cm. — (Who wrote that?)
  Includes bibliographical references and index.
  ISBN 978-1-60413-499-5 (acid-free paper) 1. Paterson, Katherine. 2. Authors, American—20th century—Biography—Juvenile literature. 3. Children's stories—Authorship—Juvenile literature. I. Title. II. Series.
  PS3566.A779Z57 2009
  813'.54—dc22
  [B]                                                    2009022345

Chelsea House books are available at special discounts when purchased in bulk quantities for business, associations, institutions, or sales promotions. Please call our Special Sales Department in New York at (212) 967-8800 or (800) 322-8755.

You can find Chelsea House on the World Wide Web at http://www.chelseahouse.com.

Text design by Keith Trego and Erika K. Arroyo
Cover design by Alicia Post
Composition by EJB Publishing Services
Cover printed by Bang Printing, Brainerd, MN
Book printed and bound by Bang Printing, Brainerd, MN
Date printed: April 2010
Printed in the United States of America

10 9 8 7 6 5 4 3 2 1

This book is printed on acid-free paper.

All links and Web addresses were checked and verified to be correct at the time of publication. Because of the dynamic nature of the Web, some addresses and links may have changed since publication and may no longer be valid.

# Table of Contents

## FOREWORD BY
# KYLE ZIMMER
### PRESIDENT, FIRST BOOK

HUMANITY IS POWERED by stories. From our earliest days as thinking beings, we employed every available tool to tell each other stories. We danced, drew pictures on the walls of our caves, spoke, and sang. All of this extraordinary effort was designed to entertain, recount the news of the day, explain natural occurrences—and then gradually to build religious and cultural traditions and establish the common bonds and continuity that eventually formed civilizations. Stories are the most powerful force in the universe; they are the primary element that has distinguished our evolutionary path.

Our love of the story has not diminished with time. Enormous segments of societies are devoted to the art of storytelling. Book sales in the United States alone topped $24 billion in 2006; movie studios spend fortunes to create and promote stories; and the news industry is more pervasive in its presence than ever before.

There is no mystery to our fascination. Great stories are magic. They can introduce us to new cultures, or remind us of the nobility and failures of our own, inspire us to greatness or scare us to death; but above all, stories provide human insight on a level that is unavailable through any other source. In fact, stories connect each of us to the rest of humanity not just in our own time, but also throughout history.

This special magic of books is the greatest treasure that we can hand down from generation to generation. In fact, that spark in a child that comes from books became the motivation for the creation of my organization, First Book, a national literacy program with a simple mission: to provide new books to the most disadvantaged children. At present, First Book has been at work in hundreds of communities for over a decade. Every year children in need receive millions of books through our organization and millions more are provided through dedicated literacy institutions across the United States and around the world. In addition, groups of people dedicate themselves tirelessly to working with children to share reading and stories in every imaginable setting from schools to the streets. Of course, this Herculean effort serves many important goals. Literacy translates to productivity and employability in life and many other valid and even essential elements. But at the heart of this movement are people who love stories, love to read, and want desperately to ensure that no one misses the wonderful possibilities that reading provides.

When thinking about the importance of books, there is an overwhelming urge to cite the literary devotion of great minds. Some have written of the magnitude of the importance of literature. Amy Lowell, an American poet, captured the concept when she said, "Books are more than books. They are the life, the very heart and core of ages past, the reason why men lived and worked and died, the essence and quintessence of their lives." Others have spoken of their personal obsession with books, as in Thomas Jefferson's simple statement: "I live for books." But more compelling, perhaps, is the almost instinctive excitement in children for books and stories.

Throughout my years at First Book, I have heard truly extraordinary stories about the power of books in the lives of children. In one case, a homeless child, who had been bounced from one location to another, later resurfaced— and the only possession that he had fought to keep was the book he was given as part of a First Book distribution months earlier. More recently, I met a child who, upon receiving the book he wanted, flashed a big smile and said, "This is my big chance!" These snapshots reveal the true power of books and stories to give hope and change lives.

As these children grow up and continue to develop their love of reading, they will owe a profound debt to those volunteers who reached out to them—a debt that they may repay by reaching out to spark the next generation of readers. But there is a greater debt owed by all of us—a debt to the storytellers, the authors, who have bound us together, inspired our leaders, fueled our civilizations, and helped us put our children to sleep with their heads full of images and ideas.

WHO WROTE THAT? is a series of books dedicated to introducing us to a few of these incredible individuals. While we have almost always honored stories, we have not uniformly honored storytellers. In fact, some of the most important authors have toiled in complete obscurity throughout their lives or have been openly persecuted for the uncomfortable truths that they have laid before us. When confronted with the magnitude of their written work or perhaps the daily grind of our own, we can forget that writers are people. They struggle through the same daily indignities and dental appointments, and they experience the intense joy and bottomless despair that many of us do. Yet somehow they rise above it all to deliver a powerful thread that connects us all. It is a rare honor to have the opportunity that these books provide to share the lives of these extraordinary people. Enjoy.

*Shown here from left are AnnaSophia Robb and Josh Hutcherson, who starred in the 2007 film version of* Bridge to Terabithia, *Katherine Paterson's beloved award-winning novel.*

# 1

# The Bridge

WHEN KATHERINE PATERSON'S son David was eight years old, he had trouble fitting in with other kids. First grade had been brutal. Now forced to attend a new school, second grade threatened to be even worse. He was artistic but friendless. While other children played, he drew pictures they called "stupid."

His mother worried. A middle child herself, Katherine Paterson knew what it was like to grow up isolated and artistic. She too found sanctuary in creating. Then one day in late autumn, David came home smiling. He had found someone to help him construct a diorama based on the Laura Ingalls Wilder classic, *Little House in the Big Woods*. Her name was Lisa Hill.

Having a female best friend still marked David as different among his peers. When she phoned, his older brother told him, "Your girlfriend's calling." The teasing never seemed to bother him. He had found someone who shared his love for art. He had found someone to share a corner with during music, both of them loudly singing "Free to Be You and Me."

"Bright, joy-filled, and self assured—the only girl to invade the second-and-third-grade T-Ball team . . . Lisa was the person you did everything with and told everything to," Katherine Paterson later recalled. "She laughed at his jokes (the ones his older brother and sister groaned over) and he laughed at hers. They played long, imaginative games in the woods behind her house and in the late spring they both turned eight years old."[1]

It was a hot August day in 1974 when the phone rang in the Paterson household. Katherine picked it up, listening "in disbelief and horror and then quickly bypassed David, reading in the living room, to search out his father. Lisa was dead. Killed by lightning on a summer afternoon."[2] Lisa Hill's death seemed the type of tragedy depicted in black-and-white movies and children's books from the early twentieth century; it did not seem possible that such a freak accident could happen in modern times. It devastated David and his mother. Already that year, Katherine had survived a bout with cancer; her son's horrific loss overwhelmed her.

"We Americans on the whole aren't very good with death," she admitted in the foreword to *Part of Me Died, Too.*

> We are all going to die, but we do everything we can to deny the fact. We parents try our best to protect our children from sorrow, and when we can't, we tell ourselves that they aren't old enough to understand death or able to feel intense loss. So,

we leave our children alone, with their questions unanswered, their grief raw and unassuaged.[3]

Lisa's grandmother, suffering from the loss, still reached out to David. She told his mother she wanted to give him a gift. A gift that might help the rawness fade, something that would allow him to heal.

David's parents decided to allow Lisa's grandmother to pay for pottery lessons. They were familiar with the potter; they knew she was kind and sensitive. Alone with her, David put his pain into the physical effort of the craft. His mood improved. By then, Katherine Paterson knew her healing would also come from creating, not with clay but with words. As a writer it was the best she could do.

By the mid-1970s, following years of rejection, Paterson had become a successful writer. The three young-adult novels she had written had won her awards and an audience. However, each of them had been set in another time and another place. She knew if she wrote this story—the story of Lisa's death and her son's loss—it would be a modern-day book set in a part of Virginia she knew well.

In 1975, she sat down at her typewriter, but "for days nothing happened," she remembered. "Finally, I said to myself, 'Okay. If you can't write what you want to, write what you can.'" She managed three pages. "I am not sure I can tell this story," she wrote. "The pain is too fresh for it to fall into rational paragraphs, but I want to try. For David, for Lisa, for Lisa's mother and for me."[4]

Katherine Paterson set those pages aside. She did not read them again for years. Instead, she returned to the thoughts they inspired. She began a novel. She wanted to capture the poetry of her young son's art and the pain of his isolation. Most of all, she wanted to sculpt a memorial in words of his friendship with Lisa.

In 1976, she submitted *Bridge to Terabithia* to her publisher. Her expectations were low. The novel did not shy away from the brutal tragedy—it was a kid's book without a happy ending. "I thought it was such a private book that my editor probably wouldn't want to publish it," she admitted in an interview in *Christianity Today*, "and if he wanted to publish it, I thought nobody would read it; and if they read it, [I thought] nobody would understand it. I was shocked to

## Did you know...

Two fantasy novels adored by generations of young readers inspired the titles of two of Katherine Paterson's books. "I thought I'd made up 'Terabithia,'" Paterson admits on her Web site. "I realized when the book was nearly done, that there is an island in *The Voyage of the Dawn Treader* by C.S. Lewis called Terebinthia. I'm sure I borrowed that unconsciously, but, then, so would Leslie who loved the *Chronicles of Narnia*. And, by the way, Lewis got Terebinthia from the Biblical terebinth tree, so it wasn't original with him either."*

Although Paterson says *Bridge to Terabithia* was an unconscious homage, she intentionally named the main character in *The Great Gilly Hopkins* after Galadriel in J.R.R. Tolkien's *The Lord of the Rings*.

* Katherine Paterson, "These Are Questions Recently Asked by Children and Educators in an Internet Interview with Katherine Paterson." Terabithia. com, http://www.terabithia.com/questions.html.

realize that teachers were reading it out loud in schools. It just seemed like a very, very private, personal story."[5]

In addition to becoming a popular best seller, *Bridge to Terabithia* won a prestigious Newbery Medal and was turned into a film in 2007. More importantly, since its publication in 1977, it has been embraced by generations of readers moved by its unabashed depiction of tragedy and abiding faith.

It was fiction, but in many ways it was not only her son's story. It was Katherine Paterson's as well. She knew what it was like to be the outsider, to sit alone at lunch and in crowded classrooms. As a child, she came home one sad February day without a single valentine. She spent the first five years of her life in China, an American in a foreign country. Yet when she returned home, she felt more like a refugee than a citizen. This is her story.

*In June 1917, French artillerymen fire English mortars during the Battle on the Somme in World War I. Katherine Paterson's father's experiences in the war led him to become a missionary to China, where his daughter was born.*

# 2

# Beginnings

*"The souvenir gatherers should be here. They could find anything from a [German] tank to cartridges and the like. I have seen so many helmets, etc., that I would like to get to a place where there are no souvenirs."[1]*

PRESERVED IN A letter home, George Womeldorf's description of the "souvenirs" from battle are more chilling when the reader realizes their significance. Every souvenir—every helmet and weapon left behind—represented a soldier, wounded or dead, who no longer needed it. During World War I (1914–1918), there were millions of both. By the time Katherine

**17**

Paterson's father wrote these words in 1918, the war was in its last year. Nearly 20 million soldiers and civilians had died across Europe. More than 55,000 Americans were killed in combat in the 18 months since the United States had entered the war.

George Womeldorf did not enlist as a solider for his country, but as a volunteer for France, the nation that had been invaded by Germany in 1914. Womeldorf grew up in Virginia's Shenandoah Valley. Recruited while he was studying at the College of William and Mary, he became an ambulance driver in the war. When he was not driving the "Tin Lizzie"—a Model T Ford—he still helped others. A fellow William and Mary volunteer recalled how, during a lull in the fighting, Womeldorf said: "See that field of wheat? There's only an old couple living on that farm. There's no one left strong enough to bring in a crop of that size. It would be a shame to let it go to waste."[2] The two young men gathered the wheat before another battle could destroy the harvest.

Carrying the wounded instead of weapons did not make Womeldorf any safer. Ferrying the injured and dying between opposing armies was no protection from lethal German artillery. Severely wounded in one such attack, he was sent home with "one leg and gas in his lungs,"[3] as his daughter Katherine Paterson remembered. Still, his desire to help others remained intact.

Womeldorf recovered. He learned to walk on an artificial leg and became a Presbyterian minister before traveling to China as a missionary. "He was, I believe, as ideally suited as any Westerner to go to China," Paterson said in a speech.

> He was intelligent, hardworking, almost fearless, absolutely stoical and amazingly humble, with the same wonderful sense of humor found in many Chinese. Not only was he capable of

learning the language and enduring the hardships of his chosen life, but he was also incapable of seeing himself in the role of Great White Deliverer.[4]

## CHILDHOOD IN CHINA

Katherine Paterson was born Katherine Anne Clements Womeldorf on Halloween, October 31, 1932. Family lore held that one of her grandfathers was related to the author Samuel Clemens, better known as Mark Twain. Today, Paterson explains how her family's genealogy (the account of her family's descendents) shows that while Twain's father "left Virginia and the 'ts' in the name without looking back, my grandfather stayed in the state until he died at age 103."[5]

By the time of her birth, her father was running a boy's school in Huaiyin, China, while her mother, Mary Elizabeth, had her hands full with the growing family. Paterson has described her place in the family as "the middle child of five, swivel position, the youngest of three older children and the oldest of three younger."[6]

The family lived on school grounds, their friends and neighbors Chinese. Katherine spoke the local language before she learned English. Most of the first years of her life were spent in China. In the United States, other children would wonder: Since Katherine was born in China, why was she not Chinese? "If a cat's born in a garage," she would reply, "does it make it an automobile?"[7]

Despite Katherine's fond childhood memories of China, the nation was disintegrating by the time the Halloween baby arrived. Only a few miles from her school, the peaceful countryside was devolving into war. More than 20 years earlier, in 1911, the Chinese Nationalist Party (also known as the Kuomintang, or KMT) overthrew the ruling Qing dynasty. The new leadership promised citizens more freedoms than they had enjoyed under dynastic rule but instead became every bit as repressive as the regime it replaced. The party's power was held by the Central Executive Committee, and everyone who belonged to it pledged to support KMT principles. Instead, they all pursued different goals for China, as if "the Democratic Party in the United States were ruled and directed by a central committee which included in its membership men and women who, while proclaiming Jeffersonian principles, were diversely made up of Democrats, Republicans, Socialists and a sprinkling of Communists,"[8] a *New York Times* reporter observed in 1928.

Despite this dysfunction, many outside of China were optimistic. The KMT seemed an improvement over the Qing dynasty. It was also viewed in Western nations like the United States and Great Britain as preferable to communism. The same reporter noted:

> A search of the old files of many American and British newspapers and magazines reveals the fact that this optimism has not only persisted but has deepened annually for the last seventeen years—seventeen years during every one of which the condition of China and of China's hundreds of millions has become annually worse.
>
> This blindness of facts is undoubtedly due at least partly to Chinese propagandists, aided to a great extent by missionaries in China, throwing immense quantities of dust for years into the eyes of the American and British peoples.[9]

Peace did not follow the KMT. Instead, Communists in China sought to overthrow their government just as Communists in Russia had in 1917. The Russian Revolution occurred fairly quickly; the one in China took decades. Indeed, a few months before Katherine was born, another

*New York Times* article predicted that "China seems destined to face a renewal of large-scale civil warfare with the coming of Spring, for neither the Kuomintang militarists nor the Communists will agree on basic compromise."[10]

That prediction was accurate—indeed "large-scale civil warfare" was hardly the worst of it. By the time Katherine was born, the province where George Womeldorf taught was the site of fierce fighting. On September 18, 1931, the Japanese invaded the Chinese province of Manchuria and established the Japanese puppet state of Manchukuo. This incident was, in fact, the opening of Japan's quest to conquer all of China and set in motion events that led to the U.S. involvement in World War II (1939–1945). But Japanese aggression in Asia—and the small island nation's quest for territory—began over 60 years earlier.

## BACKGROUND TO THE SINO-JAPANESE CONFLICT

In 1868, Japan began to pursue a policy of modernization under the Meiji Restoration, which ended shogun rule and restored the emperor to Japan. Although modeled on Western industrialization, this modernization program was hampered in Japan because the nation lacked the same natural resources as countries like the United States. Nearly everything had to be imported. Protecting trade routes led almost inevitably to warfare.

In 1895, Japan won the Sino-Japanese War. Under the terms of victory, China granted Korea independence while ceding Taiwan and the Liaodong Peninsula to Japan. This short-lived arrangement ended when France, Germany, and Russia forced Japan to abandon its toehold into China, believing it would lead to border conflicts. Instead of the move ensuring peace, Japan allied with Britain against Russia.

In 1905, Japan's victory in the Russo-Japanese War stunned the West. Russia ceded to Japan half of Sakhalin Island and exclusive rights in Korea, its concessions in Port Arthur and Dalian, and control of the South Manchuria Railway. These terms were subject to the Chinese government's approval, which Japan received in late 1905. The spoils from this war increased Japan's nationalist pride and expanded its influence in Manchuria. Five years later, Korea was formally annexed by Japan. Japan's desire for territorial expansion, however, was interrupted by World War I. Japan's alliance with the Allies against Germany was rewarded when the defeated nation gave up its Asian colonial territories: Tsingtao on the Chinese Shandong Peninsula and the Micronesian islands.

Peace lasted through the 1920s. The island nation was a player in the global economy until the Great Depression of the 1930s. In an effort to protect their declining economies, Western powers enacted harsh trade barriers, which hit Japan particularly hard. Further, in the 1920s, laws were passed in the United States restricting Japanese immigration. With their ability to import goods limited and their people's opportunities to leave curtailed, Japan's leaders renewed their quest for territory in the 1930s. The Japanese invasion of Manchuria in 1931 was "justified on the basis of the Manchurian-Mongolian seimeisen or 'lifeline' argument—the idea that Japan's economy was deadlocked," explains author Susan Townsend. "Three factors creating this deadlock loomed large—the shortage of raw materials in Japan, the rapidly expanding Japanese population, and the division of the world into economic blocs."[11]

Following the 1931 invasion, a puppet government was installed in Manchuria. Renamed Manchukuo, the region was headed by Pu Yi, the former emperor of the Qing

*Nanking Road, the principal thoroughfare in Shanghai, as seen on August 12, 1937, after a state of emergency is declared in the Chinese territory. A full-scale war broke out between China and invading Japanese forces around this time.*

dynasty, but controlled by Japan. From there, the Japanese military launched attacks to expand their territory. Over the next several years, Japan conquered regions in Inner Mongolia and other parts of northern China. Preoccupied by his battles with the Chinese Communists led by Mao Zedong, KMT leader Chiang Kai-shek consistently ceded territory to the invading Japanese. By 1934, his efforts were partly successful as his army drove the Communists from their bases in southern and central China. This focus, however, meant that even as the KMT was winning battles against internal enemies, it was losing the war against Japan.

Frustrated over the loss of territory, Manchurian soldiers kidnapped Chiang Kai-shek in 1936. They had one demand: Stop fighting the Communists and unite with them against the Japanese. He agreed. But it was too little, too late. In 1937, along the stretch of the Marco Polo Bridge near Shanghai, Chinese and Japanese troops faced off. Instead of being a minor battle, it was the beginning of a full-scale war.

This was young Katherine's childhood. She remembers low-flying planes crossing overhead on bombing runs and the sounds of distant explosions. Every year, the country became more dangerous. After the conflict at the Marco Polo Bridge, George Womeldorf decided the risk to his family was too great. The family boarded a ship (although trans-Pacific commercial flights began in 1935, they were not as common as boats for the crossing). Despite the tension, Katherine enjoyed the port stops. Every time they docked, the family visited a zoo. It was a pleasant way to forget the uncertainty of what the family faced and the dangers behind them.

## STATESIDE

Dedicated to his missionary school, George Womeldorf returned to China. The rest of his family remained in the United States. The transition was hardest on Katherine. As she entered first grade in Richmond, Virginia, she felt out of place and missed her father terribly.

Arriving in the United States, she remembers her first grade as a kind of horror. "Among the more than twice-told tales in my family is the tragic one about the year we lived in Richmond, Virginia, when I came home from first grade on February 14 without a single Valentine," she remembered. "My mother grieved over this event until her death, asking me once why I didn't write a story about the time I didn't get any valentines. 'But, Mother,' I said, 'all my stories are about the time I didn't get any valentines.'"[12] Looking back, the author admits that "my mother made a bigger deal about it than I did; I wouldn't have been so upset if she hadn't been so shocked."[13]

In 1939, the family returned to China. Life had radically changed. George traveled through enemy lines to the school. It was too dangerous for the rest of his family. They stayed behind in a number of safer cities, including Shanghai, where a cease-fire meant a relatively protected international settlement. It was a city filled with Westerners, mainly British. There, Katherine acquired a British accent, which would take years to erase, and an even more indelible fear of the Japanese.

## THE EVOLUTION OF A WRITER

"When people ask me what qualifies me to be a writer for children, I say I was once a child," Paterson later explained. "But I was not only a child, I was better still a weird little kid and . . . there are few things, apparently, more helpful to a writer than having once been a weird little kid."[14]

Although not every writer starts out as a "weird little kid," many do. Some are the children of divorce and military families, only children and lonely children, who retreat into fantasy or find conversations comfortable only with adults. Those who move frequently confront new schools occupied by new cliques, new fashions, and new slang. Surviving as chameleons by mimicking the popular kids, they often grow up being fairly good actors, able to step into another role easily. But all future writers begin as readers: Outcasts finding solace in worlds created by authors. They see their lives reflected in the tragic stories of long-dead writers like

Charles Dickens or F. Scott Fitzgerald. They find hope in books by Jane Austen and Mark Twain.

Starting out, Katherine read poems and books by A.A. Milne, famous for 1926's *Winnie-the-Pooh* and *The House at Pooh Corner* two years later. She also enjoyed Kenneth Grahame's *The Wind in the Willows* but admits that "one of the most formative books of my childhood was [Frances Hodgson] Burnett's *The Secret Garden*. I hardly know any female writers of my generation who weren't deeply influenced by *The Secret Garden*."[15]

Paterson is not sure of the exact date she began writing. But she knows she began reading by her fifth birthday and writing soon after. Like most writers, Katherine began by imitating. She rewrote the then-popular Elsie Dinsmore stories, which Paterson describes as featuring "a pious Victorian child whose mother was dead and whose father was

## Did you know...

Frances Hodgson Burnett's novel *The Secret Garden* was published in 1909 but sold poorly until after she died in 1924; most obituaries focused on her other novel, *Little Lord Fauntleroy*. Yet in the 1930s, *The Secret Garden* gained a wider audience, including Katherine Paterson and, a few years later, fellow young-adult author Lois Lowry, who is perhaps best known for her novel *The Giver*. Lowry, like Paterson, moved as a result of World War II and fell in love with the book as a young girl. Today, both authors have read their favorite Burnett novel to their grandchildren.

an unfeeling unbeliever."[16] "Fortunately, very few samples of my early writing survived the eighteen moves I made before I was eighteen years old," she confessed on Penguin Publishing's Web site. "I say fortunately, because the samples that did manage to survive are terrible."[17]

Although most writers are their own worst critics, Paterson found one thing from her amateur work worth preserving. While her father was in dangerous territory, seven-year-old Katherine wrote him a letter. She told him she missed him terribly, and in her childish words she conveyed deep emotion, the same emotional power her books would later have. Her first published piece of work came when Katherine was seven years old and her school newspaper, the *Shanghai American*, published one of her poems. By then the family realized they could not remain in China. It was far too dangerous. This time they left for good.

## NORTH CAROLINA

The Womeldorfs returned to the United States, where Katherine's father began working as a Presbyterian minister in Winston-Salem, North Carolina. Shanghai's legacy was heard whenever Katherine spoke because she now spoke English with a British accent. Even without opening her mouth, she was marked as different. She recalls she "wore clothes out of a missionary barrel. Because children are somewhat vague about geography, my classmates knew only that I had come from somewhere over there and decided if I was not a Japanese spy, certainly suspect."[18]

In late 1941, there were few things worse than being suspected of being a Japanese spy. On a quiet Sunday morning in December, Japanese forces attacked Pearl Harbor, an American naval base in Hawaii, all but destroying the U.S Pacific Fleet. This surprise attack brought the United States into World War II. Katherine was with family and friends when the announcement came over the radio. Looking back, she says, "We thought it was the end of the world."[19]

Life in North Carolina was isolating for young Katherine. "My older brother and sister were friends," the author remembers, "and my younger sisters had each other to play and quarrel with. And there I was, stranded in the middle. . . . There were plenty of bullies in my early years in the United States, but no friends—except the friends I found in books."[20] In fact, she remembers having only two real friends as a young girl. "The fourth grade was a time of almost unmitigated terror and humiliation for me," Paterson recalls. "I recognize now that some of my best writing had its seeds in that awful year. But I can't remember once saying to myself at nine, 'Buck up, old girl, someday you're going to make a mint out of this misery.'"[21]

The first friend she remembers, Eugene Hammett, was a fellow outcast. Circumstances conspired to make Katherine an outsider, but Eugene did all he could to be different. His clothes and speech were affected, whereas Katherine worked hard to fit in, even developing a southern drawl that endured for decades. Perhaps oddest of all, Eugene wanted to be a ballet dancer when he grew up. This was an incredibly uncommon goal for a young boy in that time and place. And his dreams came true: He became a successful dancer in New York City. Katherine's childhood dreams were less concrete: "When I was ten, I wanted to be either a movie star or a missionary."[22]

She did not dream of actually having a career as a writer until well into adulthood. In the library of Calvin H. Wiley School, she formed the second notable friendship of her childhood with the school librarian. To young Katherine the library was almost as sacred a place as church; the librarian as powerful as her minister father. She says, "I do not believe it would be hyperbolic to say that it saved my sanity."[23]

Looking back, Paterson cannot minimize the impact of words and books on her life. For her, reading *The Secret Garden* was more than just escapism. Paterson explains:

> A book can give a child a way to learn to value herself, which is the start of the process of growing a great soul. It is why I struggle so against the idea that characters in novels should be role models. Role models may inspire some children—but they didn't inspire any child that I ever was. They only discouraged me. Whereas that awful, bad-tempered, selfish Mary Lennox— who could admire her? Who could love such an unlovable creature? Yet she was given the key to a secret garden. Not because she deserved it but because she needed it. When I read *The Secret Garden*, I fell in love with Mary Lennox. She was my soul mate. And because I loved her, I was able to love myself a bit.[24]

## FINDING HER VOICE

By the time she was in late elementary school, Katherine was not only reading books written for her age group but also adult novels, such as *A Tale of Two Cities* by Charles Dickens and *Cry, the Beloved Country* by Alan Paton. In fifth grade, Katherine discovered how to use her budding writing talent to make friends. She wrote parts for them! Writing plays gave her an opportunity to escape the occasionally lonely internal life of a reader and writer. Although she did not suddenly become an extrovert, she was able to interact more with her peers and even gave herself an acting role. "I was very verbal and started writing plays," she later told an interviewer. "The kids respected this. I loved acting and was the evil fairy in *Sleeping Beauty*."[25]

Her classmates performed the plays on the playground and during rainy recesses when they could not go outside. "I loved those plays," the author admitted on her Web site. "I was a very shy child who loved to show off. Still am."[26] The acting fit neatly with her early dreams of movie stardom, but her plays' success with her peers did not make her want to be a writer. Instead, she became "an ad-hoc writer,"[27] crafting plays in junior high and high school whenever her classmates asked for them.

Throughout her academic career, moving was a constant. Katherine attended numerous schools, including Chandler Junior High in West Virginia and Thomas Jefferson High School in Richmond. She spent just over a year in Winchester, Virginia, before graduating from Charles Town High School. Ironically, her father would live there for the rest of his life. While his moving ended, Katherine's continued.

In 1950, Katherine enrolled at King College in Bristol, Tennessee, which is a twin city of Bristol, Virginia. (The two towns—and states—are divided by State Street.) Founded in 1867 by Holston Presbytery, the Presbyterian-affiliated college is named in honor of the Reverend James King. There, Katherine was given even more of a chance to read than she had in high school. "I spent four years at King College in Bristol, Tennessee, doing what I loved best—reading English and American Literature and avoiding math whenever possible,"[28] she admitted on the Penguin Publishing Web site. Her undergraduate reading only made her want to read more. Despite this, she still did not want to write.

For Katherine, one author stood out above all others: C.S. Lewis, whose *The Chronicles of Narnia* has enthralled

*A circa 1960 photo of British author C.S. Lewis, whose Narnia
series Katherine Paterson has loved since her childhood.*

generations. She even shared them with her friends. Standing in the aisle of a bus headed for Atlanta, she read the first volume, *The Lion, the Witch and the Wardrobe*, to her fellow students. She read until she could read no more. Her voice became a throaty whisper. Too bad they were going to a chorus competition!

In elementary school, her writing had begun as imitation. In college, the trait was more pronounced, only now she was imitating William Shakespeare, Sophocles, and poet Gerard Manley Hopkins (she would eventually borrow his last name for the main character in *The Great Gilly Hopkins*.) "We always worry that we are copying someone else, that we don't have our own style," explains Natalie Goldberg in *Writing Down the Bones*. "Don't worry. Writing is a communal act. . . . We are very arrogant to think that we alone have a totally original mind. We are carried on the backs of the writers who came before us. We live in the present with all the history, ideas and soda pop of the time. It all gets mixed up in our writing."[29]

"Indeed, an English professor once noted my chameleonic tendency to adopt the style of whatever literary figure I happened to be doing a paper on," Paterson explained in *Gates of Excellence*. "I am grateful that he encouraged me to write papers on only the best. An apprenticeship imitating the masters of the English language was bound to have a beneficial effect."[30]

Despite this, she never considered writing to be a suitable career at the time. In the 1950s, most people believed there was really only one suitable aspiration for a young middle-class woman: getting married and raising a family. Careers, if they occurred at all, occurred before marriage. After marriage, most women became housewives. Katherine's dreams were no different from her peers. When Katherine graduated summa cum laude from King College in 1954 with an A.B. degree, her youthful dreams of movie stardom had disappeared. She imagined she would still like to be a missionary. However, her ultimate goal was to "be married with lots of children."[31] Less than 10 years later, that dream would come true.

*A recent photo of an ancient castle in Nagoya, Japan. Paterson's experiences as a missionary in Japan in the 1950s helped her overcome biases she had developed years earlier while dealing with the invading Japanese army in China.*

# **3**

# **Material**

KATHERINE WOMELDORF PAUSED in a hallway at the Presbyterian School of Christian Education, where she was pursuing her master's degree. One of her favorite teachers had just stopped her to ask an important question: Had she ever considered being a writer?

" 'No,' I replied, swelling with twenty-four-year-old pomposity. 'I wouldn't want to add another mediocre writer to the world,'" Katherine Paterson later recalled.

" 'But maybe that's what God is calling you to be.' She meant of course that if I wasn't willing to risk mediocrity, I'd never accomplish anything."[1]

Paterson laughingly admits that she and Dr. Sara Little have different versions of that hallway conversation. It was difficult to imagine that God would want her to be a poor writer, but what Little meant is that "you have to start somewhere."[2]

Although few people are great their first day on the job, no one faces an empty computer screen or a blank page and decides to create something terrible. Most writers dream of producing classics that will charm critics, masterpieces that become best sellers and last for centuries. At the very least, they want someone, somewhere to like their book. Few writers start out with anything *other* than mediocre prose, explains Anne Lamott in her book on writing, *Bird by Bird*:

> People tend to look at successful writers, writers who are getting their books published and maybe even doing well financially, and think that they sit down at their desks every morning, feeling like a million dollars, feeling great about who they are and how much talent they have and what a great story they have to tell; that they take a few deep breaths, push back their sleeves, roll their necks a few times to get the cricks out, and dive in, typing fully formed passages as fast as a court reporter. But this is just the fantasy of the uninitiated. I know some very great writers, writers you love who write beautifully and have made a great deal of money, and not *one* of them sits down routinely feeling wildly enthusiastic and confident. Not one of them writes elegant first drafts.[3]

Although Lamott's passage was written long after Paterson became a successful author, Paterson says even today *Bird by Bird*'s advice is liberating. Despite working as an author for decades, she still views most of her first drafts as terrible. She frets about the quality of her work and believes only multiple revisions produce the novels for which she is famous. In the late 1950s, the future author owned a well-honed imagination but could not imagine writing something shelved beside the great works of literature. If she could not accomplish that, she thought, why bother?

Eventually, she did just that, penning a novel that has earned a place beside young-adult books she loved as a girl. In 1954, she began its research. She just did not realize it.

## TEACHING

As a sixth-grade teacher in rural Lovettsville, Virginia, Paterson gained the experiences that would inform a novel she wrote two decades later. It gave her more than a setting and students to base characters on. It was responsible for many of the emotions she captured in *Bridge to Terabithia*.

In Lovettsville, many of her students were the offspring of struggling farmers. Others had fathers who drove long distances to work construction jobs in Richmond or Washington, D.C. Herself a child of a rural area, Katherine empathized with her students. Yet in many ways she was exotic to them.

Paterson was the only teacher who had graduated college; her associates had only a two-year teaching certificate. Paterson had lived abroad for many years; many of her students had never left the county. Her youngest student was 10, her oldest 16—a very wide age range in a single class. "There was no social promotion in those days," explains the author. Children who did not pass sixth-grade courses repeated until they did. Still, she refuses to admit that anyone in her class was remotely similar to the ones who once teased her during her own childhood. "Oh, they were all Jesse Aarons,"[4] Paterson laughs, referring to *Bridge to Terabithia*'s sensitive main character.

Being different as an adult helped her to understand how being different as a child often made one's peers feel threatened because they generally had little exposure to places more than a few miles away. In *Bridge to Terabithia*, she modeled music teacher Miss Edmund's experiences on challenges Paterson herself confronted in Lovettsville. As an outsider, she did all she could to open up the world for her students. Just two years later, the world opened up for Paterson. She just was not sure if she was prepared.

## MISSIONARY IN JAPAN

In 1955, Paterson challenged her students to overcome their prejudices. Two years later, she found herself challenging prejudices of her own. After graduating from the Presbyterian School with a master's degree in Christian education in 1957, she could have continued teaching in the United States. Instead, she wanted to fulfill a girlhood dream "to be a missionary to China and eat Chinese food three times a day."[5]

### Did you know...

Years after *Bridge to Terabithia* was published, one of Paterson's former students read about the book and realized it was based on her class in Lovettsville, Virginia. By that time, the student was already a grandmother (although Paterson notes most of her students married younger than she did). The author says she later had a small reunion with some of her Lovettsville students.

That dream, however, could not be accomplished in 1957. Since the Communist takeover in 1949, China was far less welcoming to outsiders, especially those with religious backgrounds. Under the new Communist regime, Chinese students were taught not to believe in God or religion. However, the Presbyterian Church did have an opportunity for her: Would she consider teaching in Japan?

She would be able to be a missionary, fulfilling a dream. The opportunity was inviting, but her memory of the Japanese was immobilizing. "I remember the Japanese as an occupying army," Paterson explained in a 1977 speech. "The Japanese soldiers came screaming up the beach and across our yard in Tsingtao, practicing, they said, for the invasion of San Francisco."[6]

Yet Japan had changed considerably since it lost World War II in 1945. As she later recalled:

> What made it possible for me to go to Japan at all was a close friend I had in graduate school, a Japanese pastor who persuaded me that despite the war, I would find a home in Japan if I would give the Japanese people a chance. And she was right. In the course of four years, I was set fully free from my deep, childish hatred. I truly loved Japan.[7]

Like her father, Paterson's Presbyterian missionary experience meant teaching school. After earning her M.A., she left for Nashville, Tennessee, and the Presbyterian Church Board of World Missions. Educated there about what it meant to be a missionary, she then left for Japan.

Since Japan's 1945 surrender, the country had to abandon the territory acquired before and during World War II. In the 1940s, Allied forces led by the U.S. general, Douglas MacArthur, occupied Japan and its former territories. During the occupation, Japan was put on the path to democracy by American officials, who helped the Japanese draft a constitution guaranteeing free elections. The emperor retained his title, but not his power. The new Japanese constitution was ratified in 1947; five years later the occupation ended (although the United States still maintains a military base in Okinawa). In 1956, Japan joined the United Nations.

Devastated by the war, Japanese industry grew from the ruins. By the time Paterson arrived in 1957—just a dozen years after the surrender—hundreds of factories were running, many of them more modern than their American counterparts. This was the economic foundation that led to the country becoming a world leader in electronics and automobiles.

"I went to live in Japan when I was twenty-four," the author remembered, "and I became a child again, for I was not only illiterate, but unable to speak or understand. This time the Japanese taught me things the soldiers on the beach had not. The violence has always been there, but so has the beauty."[8]

The Naganuma School of Japanese Language in Kōbe, Japan, offered her an education in the country's native tongue. While she continued language training there, the future author had learned enough by the end of 1957 to begin teaching. She worked as a Christian-education assistant to 11 pastors on Shikoku Island. Despite the differences in language and culture, the school where she taught was rural like the school in Virginia. It was a country filling up with modern apartments and office buildings, yet she lived in a home without hot water. While her experiences in Lovettsville would eventually provide her with the setting for a novel, Japan's feudal history would offer her enough material for a trilogy.

In Japan, the modern and the ancient sometimes blend. The Nagoya Castle is located in Kōbe, not far from where Paterson received her Japanese language instruction. This five-story structure, constructed in 1612 for the Tokugawa clan, was destroyed during World War II. Yet during her time there, it was completely rebuilt, the replica being nearly identical to the original. Bombs could not eradicate ancient traditions or the stories first told over a thousand years before. "When you live in Japan you can't help but notice the history,"[9] Paterson explains, describing a country where some temples survived for a millennia.

Spending her first years in a foreign country and then living among Americans she felt little kinship with made the adjustment easier. In Japan, she became very comfortable. "I had every intention of spending the rest of my life among the Japanese,"[10] Paterson later confessed on her publisher's Web site. Instead, an opportunity arose that radically altered her life's direction.

## JOHN BARSTOW PATERSON

In 1961, she was accepted into the Union Theological Seminary in New York. The program gave her more than a second master's degree. It also introduced her to her future husband.

John Barstow Paterson was a Presbyterian minister from Buffalo, New York, enrolled in the same program as Katherine. She was approaching 30 and not looking for a husband. Indeed, her plans and the plans of the church that sponsored her were for her to return to Japan after she completed the course work. So what was it about the minister that convinced her to give up those dreams and get married? "Persistence," she laughs, adding, "and he was very attractive."[11]

They met in February 1962 and married on July 14 of the same year—and part of that time he was a minister in Buffalo. That same year, Katherine earned her second master's degree. For a while she continued her nomadic lifestyle, always moving from place to place. Katherine worked for a while as a substitute teacher, a job she hated, before being hired to teach English and sacred studies at the Pennington School for Boys in New Jersey. It was there that her first son, John Barstow Paterson Jr., was born in 1965. Six months later, the Patersons adopted their first daughter, Elizabeth Po Lin, who had been born in Hong Kong.

## SETTLING INTO WRITING

In 1966, the Paterson family's constant travel ceased when they settled in Tacoma Park, Maryland, where they would live for over a decade. Perhaps the stability helped Paterson take more time to write, but when she arrived in Maryland, she was already an author. "I suppose my life as a writer began in 1964," she explained on the Penguin Publishing Web site.

> The Presbyterian Church asked me to write some curriculum materials for fifth and sixth grade. Since the Church had given me a scholarship to study and I had married instead of going back to work in Japan, I felt I owed them something for their money. So I began writing. By the time the books were published, I had moved three more times, acquired three children, and was hooked on writing.[12]

Indeed, this first writing assignment had come from the same person who had challenged her in a hallway half a dozen years before: Dr. Sara Little. The obligation allowed her to see herself as more than just a housewife. Her husband encouraged this. "He believed that I could write during all those years that no one wanted to publish anything I had written," Paterson said of her husband in an interview on her official Web site, Terabithia.com. "He was the one who made me put 'writer' on the IRS form instead of 'housewife.' He is my first editor and my best reader. And no matter what I say, he always thinks that I can write another book."[13] (Her husband's initial editorial advice eventually led to their collaborations on two books: 1986's *Consider the Lilies: Plants of the Bible* and 1998's *Images of God*. Both were written for middle readers, the same audience as her fiction.)

John Paterson also gave Katherine her first real audience, his congregation, when he read her work to them. Even her earliest work had elements of fiction: story structure, characters, and vivid description. These early stories would be published in collections decades later: *Angels and Other Strangers* in 1979 and *A Midnight Clear* in 1995. Both represent the fledgling author's first efforts to write stories younger audiences might appreciate.

As Paterson was beginning to hone her literary instincts, her family was growing. She and John adopted their next daughter, Mary, who was born on an Apache reservation, in 1966; David, their last "homemade" baby, as Paterson calls him, was born the same year. Four children could have provided an excuse for Paterson to stop writing, but she did not take it. "Very often people ask me, 'How do you find time to write?'" the author commented. "I realized that the questioner was assuming that my husband's work and my children's activities were limitations that enslaved me, whereas I felt they were the very boundaries that gave form to my life."[14]

The work on fifth- and sixth-grade curriculum guides gave her a first taste of being an author. Her first book, *Who*

*Am I?*, a nonfiction religious work, was published in 1966. This led to other writing jobs, all nonfiction and religious. Every time she completed a work of nonfiction, she spent time on short stories and poetry, which she sent to numerous potential publishers with little success. She realized being a published author was not enough. "I decided I didn't want to write nonfiction. I wanted to write what I love to read— fiction. I didn't know that wanting to write fiction and being able to write fiction were two quite separate things."[15]

In his book *On Writing*, author Stephen King advises aspiring novelists: "If you happen to be a science fiction fan, it's natural that you should want to write science fiction. . . . If you're a mystery fan, you'll want to write mysteries, and if you enjoy romances, it's natural for you to want to write romances of your own."[16]

Certainly, Paterson, wanting to write young-adult fiction, could draw inspiration from the books she read to her children. There were also the books she had read as a child, some of which she reread and others of which subconsciously inspired her. As a woman in her thirties, she picked up books for middle readers. She read Madeleine L'Engle's Newbery-winning *A Wrinkle in Time*. Later she enjoyed M.E. Kerr's *Is That You Miss Blue* and regrets missing teenage author S.E. Hinton's 1967 best-selling debut, *The Outsiders*. Still, there was one book she read more than any other—her dog-eared copy of *The Heike Story* by Eiji Yoshikawa, which she still owns.

Published in 1956, this modern translation of a thirteenth century tale describes the battles between the Heike and Genji clans. The novel depicts the rise to power of Kiyomori of the Heike clan; in Japan, the source material is considered one of the most important of all the war tales. From its opening lines about the fleeting nature of human existence to its focus on the defeated and karmic retribu-tion, the book reveals a philosophy that runs counter to what is found in many Western texts.

The complex story was an inspiration to a writer like Paterson who wanted to write complicated novels. Between the short stories she submitted, the nonfiction work she was paid for, and "in the cracks of time between feedings, dia-pering, cooking, reading aloud, walking to the park, getting still another baby, and carpooling to nursery school, I wrote and wrote, and published practically nothing."[17]

Yet Paterson still managed to pinch off a minute here, a minute there, until she had a decent pile of short stories and poems. She says, "I was feeling the need of something at the end of the day that had not been eaten up, soiled or taken apart at the hands of a curious toddler."[18] Despite the intense labor, she enjoyed only two sales of her creative work over the course of seven years. "The first was a short story to a Roman Catholic magazine which folded immedi-ately thereafter, and the second was a poem that I sold for ten dollars to another small magazine, which folded before my poem could be published,"[19] she recalls.

Paterson was discouraged, until "a friend in the church . . . felt sorry for me," she told the Penguin Web site. "There I was . . . trying to write with no success. So she decided to take me to an adult education course in creative writ-ing once a week."[20] The discipline of regularly producing fiction for her classmates had an amazing effect—the act itself eliminated her stress. Then, in the late 1960s, Paterson began to work on a novel.

Katherine Paterson is photographed around the time she earned a "Puppet's Choice" award from Kids on the Block–Vermont, one of the many awards she has received throughout her career. In the late 1960s, when she was completing work on her first novel, such success seemed almost unimaginable.

# 4

# Breakthrough

"YEARS AGO WHEN I was trying to learn how to write fiction, I made up a motto for myself that would run through my head like a mantra," Katherine Paterson recalled in a 1994 speech. *"Something's got to happen. Someone's got to change. In books for children, the someone who must change is, of course, the young protagonist."*[1]

Every week, Paterson attended the adult education course. Her group was focused on writing books for young adults—and so was Paterson. She told herself writing a chapter a week was no harder than writing a short story a week—something she had already done. In a few months, she would have a completed novel.

Setting a goal and achieving it are two different things. The book progressed in fits and starts. Novels are generally more than a series of connected short stories. She needed a character the reader could follow throughout, a character that changed in a believable way. "After I returned to the States," Paterson explained, "I began writing about Japan because I missed being there, and I set my stories in the past because it is easier to see patterns there than in the present."[2]

Twelfth-century Japan was the canvas on which Paterson painted stories with modern dilemmas—like accepting a new baby brother, or seeking an absent father—and ancient solutions. The epic power struggles between rival clans the Heike and Genji provided real-life drama. She set her books against events like the Hogen Insurrection in 1159 and the Gempei War 21 years later, during which time dynasties were destroyed and a toddler emperor ascended to the throne. It was a time familiar nearly a thousand years later as the age of the noble samurai. It was also a time when the poor died by the scores and a young girl could be sold into prostitution by a greedy uncle.

Paterson worked on her first novel, *The Sign of the Chrysanthemum*, from 1968 to 1970. Finally, she felt it was ready to submit it to a publisher. She faced a daunting, almost overwhelming task. Forty years ago, like today, hundreds of manuscripts were submitted to publishers for every one published. Most of these submissions came from agents, from writers who had developed a connection within the publishing house, or from authors who graduated from the top Master of Fine Arts writing programs like the ones at the University of Iowa or the University of California at Irvine. Some had all three; Paterson had none of these going for her. But she was determined and committed to her writing—important qualities for someone looking to become a published author.

"I heard a preacher say recently that hope is a revolutionary patience; let me add that so is being a writer," explains author Anne Lamott in her book *Bird by Bird*. "Hope begins in the dark, the stubborn hope that if you show up and try to do the right thing, the dawn will come. You wait and watch and work; you don't give up."[3]

"I wrote down the names of publishers who published books I liked and sent the manuscripts to them alphabetically,"[4] Paterson recalled. The "slush pile" is the stack of manuscripts that arrive unasked for at every publishing house. Today, many publishers do not even look at these unsolicited works; those that do rely on unpaid interns or low-level editorial assistants for the job. These books each represent someone's dream, but many are fortunate if they receive even a form rejection letter.

Only occasionally does a writing contract result from such a submission. In those cases, talent, a good story, timing, and luck blend into the perfect soup. *The Sign of the Chrysanthemum* was pulled from the slush pile at the publisher Thomas Y. Crowell by editor Ann Beneduce, who liked it enough to insist that her boss take a look at it. Fortunately for Paterson, Beneduce's boss had just returned from Japan and was excited by a story set in the country.

The novel was accepted for publication and the fledgling author assigned to an editor. Virginia Buckley has since worked at several publishing houses, but Paterson has remained with her for over three decades. Noting how both her husband and editor represent long-lasting relationships, the author advises, "When a relationship works, you shouldn't be quick to give up on it."[5]

Paterson and Buckley worked together as the author labored toward becoming a published novelist. Paterson acknowledged some concern about the book's adult content,

*An ink-on-paper illustration of the Heiji Uprising, which occurred in Japan in 1159. The Sign of the Chrysanthemum, Paterson's first novel, took place in twelfth-century Japan.*

but suspected she would get away with more in her histori-cal fiction. In her first two novels, both set in ancient Japan, a teen girl winds up in a brothel, while another marries her stepfather. Yet the scenes were never graphically written, and she laughs when she quotes a friend who says the most erotic scene in a novel was the "rocking of the carriage in *Madame Bovary*,"[6] the 1856 novel by Gustave Flaubert once prosecuted for obscenity but considered fairly tame to modern audiences.

Imagining the best while fearing the worst, many writers fret about their debut. Paterson was no different. The novel was well received; in one review it was praised by the magazine *Horn Book*:

> The storytelling holds the reader by the quick pace of the lively episodes, the colorful details, and the superb development of three important characters: the confused but sometimes quick-witted boy, the philosophical, deeply kind Master; and Takanobu, a renegade samurai warrior, now a completely amoral drifter who takes advantage of Muna's innocence.[7]

Conflict is crucial for fiction writers. Without conflict, there is no story. There are exceptions, but whether dealing with a new sibling, a new home, new parents, or any number of other situations, the main character must overcome obstacles. This allows the protagonist to evolve—and in the process learn about him- or herself and others.

Paterson notes that in *The Hero with a Thousand Faces*,

> [Author] Joseph Campbell reduces the multitude of the world's myths to a single story—that of the hero who ventures forth from the ordinary world into a realm of wonders. There he is met by a supernatural guide who aides him as he defeats fabulous forces and returns a victor, able to bestow boons [blessings or benefits] on his fellows.[8]

## FEAR OF THE SOPHOMORE SLUMP

Novelists worry about the "sophomore slump." What if their second novel is not as popular or as well reviewed as their first? First books can take years, even decades to complete. Second books are often written under contracts and deadlines. Even more daunting, Paterson admits she never knows what she is going to write about from one book to the next. When she finishes a novel, she usually fears it will be the last one she ever writes.

Still, for her next two novels, Paterson returned to familiar territory: ancient Japan. Despite taking place nearly a thousand years ago, her second novel, *Of Nightingales That Weep*, also dealt with issues familiar to modern readers. After the father of the main character, Takiko, is killed, she moves in with her mother and her new husband. Accustomed to the luxurious lifestyle of a respected samurai's daughter, she has difficulty adjusting to her stepfather's rural home. Struggling with the changes in her life, Takiko feels distant toward her stepfather. Although she begins to accept him, the emotional chasm is widened when her mother gives birth. Takiko's stepbrother sparks new jealousy. In time, Takiko's feelings for both an enemy warrior

## Did you know...

Joseph Campbell's book examining the hero's journey, *The Hero with a Thousand Faces*, has been cited by numerous authors and filmmakers as a template for their creations. One of the book's best-known devotees, George Lucas, credited it as an inspiration for *Star Wars*. A memo for Disney Studios written by Christopher Vogler, a producer and screenwriter, examined the use of the book by screenwriters. This guideline led in part to the development of the Disney movies *Aladdin*, *The Lion King*, and *Beauty and the Beast*.

and her stepfather grow increasingly mature. Her emotional conflict mirrors a greater battle raging not far from her new home. In twelfth-century Japan, two rival clans, the Heike and the Genji, battled for control of the country. This civil war swept away empires and cost thousands of lives. Among the casualties was Takiko's own father.

Paterson's historical fiction addressed common teen concerns with an uncommon technique. In the 1970s, as divorce rates increased, children increasingly lived in "blended" families. Although the circumstances leading to Takiko having a stepfather and stepbrother were radically different, the emotions were the same.

Paterson's mother and father did not divorce; she never faced step siblings or stepparents. Still, many of her novels have a core story of suffering from the loss of a parent or seeking an absent one. " 'What's with you?' I asked myself," the author reflected years later. "Why are you always looking for a lost parent? You had two perfectly good parents of your own who loved you and did the best they could for you under often difficult circumstances. Why the constant theme of searching or yearning for the absent parent?' " After some reflection, and quite a few novels, Paterson came to realize the reason "this theme keeps coming up in my books reveals a longing—not so much for my own parents—but a yearning for the One whose name is unpronounceable but whom Jesus taught us to call Father."[9]

## WRITING HISTORICAL FICTION

An uncommon setting is just one of historical fiction's advantages. Fans of this genre appreciate the well-researched novels that immerse readers in times and places that are radically different than the modern United States. (Paterson spent four years in Japan, and a decade afterward learning about the country's history.) Fictional stories with made-up characters and scenes can create a context for history. Nonfiction—from books on historical periods to biographies like this one—are bound by facts, so it is not always possible to know what the weather was like during a battle or how the average person lived.

Despite these challenges, nonfiction authors have crafted works embodying the best qualities of fiction over the last 40 years. They tell stories featuring sympathetic characters facing challenges that define them and alter their lives. Truman Capote's *In Cold Blood* set the tone for modern nonfiction. Published in 1966, it depicted the real-life events following the brutal murders of a family in Kansas in 1959. Its narrative arc, novelistic details, and compelling story were considered groundbreaking for the era. For these reasons, it is often called the first "nonfiction novel." More recent examples of such nonfiction include Erik Larson's books *The Devil in the White City* and *Thunderstruck*, which relied on original sources, including letters, diaries, and court transcripts. The results are compelling true stories with dialogue that reads like a novel.

Nevertheless, historically accurate nonfiction cannot always accomplish what a novel can. Novels can depict the lives of people who lived lives that were less documented than famous figures. In portraying such a life, novelists can provide insight into average people enduring historical changes.

What is challenging to both authors of nonfiction and historical fiction is the fact that there is less information about a period the further back in time a writer explores. Although Paterson's research on twelfth-century feudal Japan revealed quite a bit about the era, the accounts she discovered had little to say about the lives of average citizens, especially 13-year-old girls like her main character, Takiko.

Historical fiction opens up new worlds. It also educates. From *Escape from Egypt*, Sonia Levitin's story of the country in 1300 B.C., to Avi's American Revolutionary War saga, *Fighting Ground*, to Jane Yolen's *The Devil's Arithmetic*, readers appreciate both the stories and discovering unfamiliar places and cultures. Describing her debut young-adult novel, *Bewitching Season*, set in Victorian England, author Marissa Doyle admits:

> One thing that is very important to me when writing historical fiction is to try and be as true as I possibly can to the mindset of the period. I intensely dislike historical fiction that is simply 21st century people in period costumes with 21st century values and mores. . . . I wanted to be very careful to make them products of their time and social class, yet still have them be accessible to modern teen readers.[10]

*The Master Puppeteer*, Paterson's third novel, was also set in Japan, although some five centuries after her first two. Set during a famine in eighteenth-century Osaka, the story of Jiro and his best friend, Kishi, the puppet master's son, was widely praised for its intricate adventure story and faithful rendering of Japanese history. The novel gained the author both wider recognition and a prestigious National Book Award. Yet by the time she received the prize in 1977, she had already moved away from writing historical fiction.

When a writer's novels all fit into a specific genre, publishing one that does not is risky. The horror novelist who attempts literary fiction, the literary award winner who crafts a science fiction novel, both face the same dilemma. What happens if their loyal readers abandon them, while readers of the genre they are attempting to enter ignore their efforts?

Paterson knew what she faced. Yet in the mid-1970s, she did not see a choice. Tragedy had struck her family. The best path to recovery was telling its story.

*Katherine Paterson won the Newbery Medal—which is given yearly by the Association for Library Service to Children to the author of the most distinguished contribution to American children's literature—for* Bridge to Terabithia *in 1978.*

# 5

# Unhappy Inspiration

FOR KATHERINE PATERSON, the spring of 1974 at first seemed a season of promise. Four years later, she recalled:

> I was forty-one years old with a husband and four children whom I loved very much, my first novel published, and a second soon to be, with a third bubbling along, friends I cared about in a town I was delighted to live in, when it was discovered that I had cancer. I could not in any justice cry, "Why me?" for no one had been given more of the true wealth of the world than I.[1]

There were difficult times, but by the end of the summer, Paterson's prognosis was good. She had scarcely celebrated

when her family endured darker and more permanent tragedy. Her eight-year-old son David's best friend, Lisa Hill,
was killed by lightning.

After Lisa's death, David's grieving was profound. He
began believing Lisa had not died for her own sins (for she
had been good) but for his. He was certain God would take
everyone he loved. His mother noted wryly that she was
number two on the list, after his sister Mary.

In January 1975, Paterson attended a nearby meeting of
the Children's Book Guild of Washington, D.C. David was
slowly healing, the grieving process helped by pottery lessons provided by a kindly teacher. Still, her son's pain was
on her mind when "by some chance or design, depending on
your theology," she was placed at the head table with Dutton
Books editor Ann Durell. Before the meeting, the author
exchanged pleasantries with the others. She was asked how
her children were and "the answer, as we all know, is 'Fine.'
But I botched it. Before I could stop myself I began to *really*
tell how the children were, leading my startled tablemates
into the story of David's grief." When she finished, everyone was silent, rendered speechless by her narrative. Then,
Durell spoke. "I know this sounds just like an editor, but
you should write that story. Of course, the child can't die by
lightning. No editor would believe that."[2]

A few days later, in her office, Paterson began to work.
She picked up a half-used spiral notebook and a pencil. She
was not ready for a fresh notebook. She did not want to
type. Despite the editor's encouragement, she was certain
the story would come to nothing. At the very least it did not
feel like a book for young adults. What she was writing was
unlike anything she had ever written. It was more therapy
than literature.

Eventually she typed up what she had scribbled in pencil. A story emerged, but that did not make her feel any better. In fact, with every completed page, she felt more depressed. Setting them aside, she found other things to do.

Procrastination is often as big a part of a writer's toolbox as grammar and dialogue. Paterson cleaned her kitchen. She answered letters. She rearranged her bookshelves. Until one day she met with a friend who asked the magic words: How was the new book coming? Paterson looked her friend in the eye and admitted, "I'm writing a book in which a child dies, and I can't let her die. I guess I can't face going through Lisa's death again." The author later recalled her friend's response: "'Katherine,' she said, looking me in the eye, for she is a true friend, 'I don't think it's Lisa's death you can't face. I think it's yours.'"[3]

Her friend's honesty inspired Paterson. It did not make the work easier. Writers joke about their best work as "opening a vein." For Paterson, that was not far from the truth. "I went straight home to my study and closed the door," the author admitted. "If it was my death I could not face, then by God, I would face it. I began in a kind of fever, and in a day I had written the chapter, and within a few weeks I had completed the draft, the cold sweat pouring down my arms."[4] (Although she wrote that first draft quickly, she notes today, "I love to re-write. First drafts are usually painful. But a good re-write morning is bliss."[5]) When she finished—the novel in progress had a beginning, middle, and end—the author did something she had not done before or since. "It was not a finished book, and I knew it, but I went ahead and did what no real writer would ever do: I had it typed up and mailed it off to Virginia [Buckley] before the sweat had a chance to evaporate."[6]

Like most writers, Paterson is convinced there is "no span of time quite so eternal as that between the mailing of the manuscript and the reception of an editor's reply," and like many writers she spent that time convinced her editor hated it. Buckley did not hate it; in fact, she "laughed through the first two thirds and cried through the last." It needed work—reflecting Paterson's motto that *someone's got to change*, the editor pointed out that while Jesse went through changes, Leslie needed to as well. Ann Beneduce thought Paterson needed to convince readers that Jesse had an artistic mind. Paterson struggled with that concept, until one day when she asked David why he never drew scenes from nature. "I can't get the poetry of the trees,"[7] he explained with a line she borrowed for the novel and gave to Jesse Aarons.

Helped by Buckley, Beneduce, and her son, the author revised the novel. Once again, she found joy in the process; she could hardly wait to get to work each morning and regularly skipped lunch. The author remembers it "like falling happily if a little crazily in love."[8]

### BRIDGE TO TERABITHIA

*Bridge to Terabithia* told David's story through the eyes of fifth-grader Jesse. Like David, Jesse is artistic and determined. He lives in Lark Creek, a place based on Lovettsville, Virginia. The author borrowed generously from her time as a fifth-grade teacher at the rural school. Like those children, Jesse's classmates are mostly from farm families or, like Jesse, have fathers who work in construction. His dad labors long hours far from home. Without him around, Jesse feels surrounded by women: Besides his mother, he has two younger and two older sisters. Hoping to win the races held every recess between boys in his school, he spends his summer training feverously.

On the first day back, victory instead goes to Leslie. New to the school, the transplant from urban Richmond is the only girl who has ever competed. She not only beats Jesse but all the other boys as well. Her "radical" perspective marks her as an outsider. It is something Jesse has in common with her; for his secret love of drawing and art makes him different from his peers. Despite this common bond, he resents losing the important race to a girl.

Off to a challenging start, their friendship is slow to form. This was just one of many realistic details in the novel. Eventually the two "outsiders" become friends. They cultivate a secret haven in the woods where they rule as king and queen. They call it "Terabithia."

Paterson was inspired by her son David's imaginative games with Lisa. In the novel, Leslie's death from drowning was as unexpected and heartwrenching as Lisa's, and Jesse's pain as permanent as her son's. "Now it was time for him to move out," Paterson writes of Jesse, when he thought about the place where he and his best friend had once ruled an imaginary kingdom. "She wasn't there, so he must go for both of them. It was up to him to pay back the world in beauty and caring what Leslie had loaned him in vision and strength."[9]

The book attracted numerous positive reviews. Jack Forman, in *School Library Journal*, described it as "an unromantic, realistic, and moving reaction to a personal tragedy."[10] Writing of the novel three decades later, the editors of the same magazine conceded that "critics said kids couldn't cope with a story about a boy named Jesse who learns to deal with the death of his best friend, Leslie. But Paterson proved them wrong."[11]

*Bridge to Terabithia*'s tragic conclusion worried adults more than its intended audience. That is because younger readers often encounter death both in novels written for them and in adult works they discover. For example, *The Yearling*, Marjorie Kinnan Rawlings's 1939 Pulitzer Prize–winning novel, was never intended for children. Yet it has inspired generations who have been captivated by the over-400-page story. In Rawlings's novel, the main character is approaching his teens and takes care of an unusual pet: a deer. The presence of the deer helps make the work naturally appealing to a younger audience. Yet the book also filled with tragedy and heartbreak. It is a story that is rough and coarse and sometimes ugly, like life itself.

## Did you know...

In 1985, *Bridge to Terabithia* was turned into a television movie by PBS. Both fans of the novel and the author were generally disappointed. "I liked the book better," Paterson recalls one fan saying, "because in the book you knew what Jesse was thinking and how he was feeling." Shortly after the TV version, Paterson accepted an opportunity to adapt the novel for the stage. She took the job "because I thought I might be able to do a better adaptation than the filmmakers had." With the help of cowriter Stephanie Tolan and composer Steven Liebman, she solved the problem of letting the audience know what the characters were thinking by having them sing their thoughts.*

* Katherine Paterson, *The Invisible Child: On Reading and Writing Books for Children*. Dutton Children's Books: New York, 2001, p. 44.

*Katherine Paterson's Newbery Medal was just the first of many awards. Here she plays with her dog Annie at her home in Barre, Vermont, on March 15, 2006, shortly after learning she had won the Astrid Lindgren Memorial Award for Literature given by the Swedish government. The $640,000 prize is the largest international award dedicated to writers of children's books.*

*The Yearling*'s conclusion has been quoted in speeches by both Paterson and her contemporary, author Lois Lowry: "He did not believe he should ever again love anything, man or woman or his own child, as he had loved the yearling. He would be lonely all his life. But a man took it for his share and went on."[12] Like Paterson, Lowry discovered the book as a young girl. Both writers see the power and necessity of endings that may not be happy but are absolutely honest.

"We choose to write not what is fashionable or what we think may sell but what comes out of our deepest selves—the sounds of our own particular hearts," Paterson offered in a 2003 article. "The writer is not responsible for how readers will respond to her story. She cannot—indeed she does not wish to control their response to what she has written. It is a part of the writer's reverence for all of life. A novelist doesn't have the luxury of despising any life—whether it be on the page or off."[13]

*Bridge to Terabithia* achieved a level of success of which most writers can only dream. More than 30 years after its publication, the novel remains Paterson's best-selling work. She honors it by naming her Web site Terabithia.com. In 1978, the book won the Newbery Medal from the American Library Association. The association's Web site notes that the medal is awarded every year "for the most distinguished American children's book published the previous year. On June 22, 1921, Frederic G. Melcher proposed the award to the American Library Association and suggested that it be named for the eighteenth-century English bookseller John Newbery." The medal's purpose is to "encourage original creative work in the field of books for children. To emphasize to the public that contributions to the literature for children deserve similar recognition to poetry, plays, or novels. To give those librarians, who make it their life work to serve children's reading interests, an opportunity to encourage good writing in this field."[14] The Newbery Award thus became the first children's book award in the world.

Although the award gave Paterson enormous professional success, it is clear from *Bridge to Terabithia*'s dedication why she intended to write it: "I wrote this book for my son David Lord Paterson, but after he read it he asked me to put Lisa's name on this page as well, and so I do. For David Paterson and Lisa Hill, banzai."[15] In her speech at the Newbery

Awards, Katherine Paterson explained the meaning of the Japanese word *banzai*:

> The two characters that make up the word say "all years," but the word itself combines the meanings of our English word "Hooray" with the ancient salute to royalty, "Live forever!" It is a cry of triumph and joy, a word full of hope in the midst of the world's contrary evidence.... It is a word that I think Leslie Burke would have liked.[16]

Paterson, like dozens of Newbery winners before her, felt liberated. The prize was empowering. It seemed to give her permission to continue taking risks as a writer. The young characters in her Japanese trilogy faced the same emotions as Paterson had growing up. *Bridge to Terabithia* and the books that followed it reflected settings, situations, and emotions from her own life. Indeed, it was during her struggle to complete and revise *Terabithia* when circumstances thousands of miles away inspired her next work.

*Mobs of Vietnamese scale the walls of the U.S. embassy in Saigon in an effort to get to helicopter pick-up zones as the capital of South Vietnam falls to North Vietnamese forces on May 1, 1975.*

# 6

# The Forgotten and Discarded

IN THE EARLY days of May 1975, the last Americans were evacuated out of Saigon, South Vietnam. The long U.S. military involvement in Southeast Asia was coming to an end. In just over a week, U.S. planes evacuated nearly 40,000 Americans and refugees from South Vietnam. The American presence ended with a few dozen helicopters landing and taking off two at a time from tennis courts beside the Tan Son airport. Nearby, terrified crowds of Vietnamese hoping to be taken from the country surrounded the U.S. embassy.

"The last days of the evacuation were very hairy indeed," President Gerald R. Ford confessed afterward in *Time*'s May

12, 1975, issue. "We were never sure whether we were going to have trouble with the mobs." The article went on to note that "the U.S. presence in Viet Nam can be said to have ended last Wednesday morning at 7:52 local time when a helicopter pilot radioed the final official message from Saigon: 'Swift 22 is airborne with eleven passengers. Ground-security force is aboard.'"[1]

The U.S. involvement in the Vietnam War had stretched over a decade. By the time it concluded, more than 50,000 Americans had died, along with hundreds of thousands of Vietnamese, and the conflict had spread from Vietnam to Laos and Cambodia. As the United States pulled out, supporters of the war against Communist North Vietnam were executed. Thousands of children were left homeless. Their images populated the nightly news.

In the Paterson living room, her children were asking, "Can't we help? Don't we have room for some more children?" At first their mother responded, "I can't take care of more than four children. We can't possibly afford another child."[2]

Katherine Paterson considered a compromise. Permanently adopting a child did not seem possible, but she could take in foster children. The author felt qualified and prepared when she agreed to take in two Cambodian boys for two weeks. She was wrong.

"We bought a bunk bed so we could turn the boy's bedroom into a dormitory," she remembered in a 1983 speech, "and I started cooking rice three times a day, thinking how lucky these boys were to come into the home of a woman who knew how to cook rice properly. Well, it wasn't as easy as cooking rice." Two weeks stretched into four; one month into two. Paterson felt she was "a B- or at the least a C+ mother, and here I was flunking."[3]

Then, she realized why. Her children, both natural and adopted, were forever. There was no going back. Problems had to be addressed, not ignored or walked away from. Paterson recalled:

> Thank heavens this is only temporary! And what I was doing was regarding another human being as a disposable commodity. Now I am quite aware that there is nothing funny about this attitude. I am also aware of the thousands of foster children in this country who have to live out their lives in a world that regards them as disposable and it took me quite a while to realize that the funny book I wanted to write was buried in this tragic idea.[4]

Paterson was inspired to name the main character in *The Great Gilly Hopkins* after a character in a Tolkien novel. In college, when a friend recommended J.R.R. Tolkien's *The Lord of the Rings* trilogy, Paterson was too busy. The summer after her two foster children found permanent homes, she read the books. After the challenges of foster care and rewriting *Terabithia*, the novels were ideal. Transported to the mythical realm of Frodo and Sam's adventures, Paterson forgot her worries. She sometimes even forgot where she was! Finishing the final volume, *The Return of the King*, Paterson remembers:

> I looked up from Sam's last words, startled to find myself in a bathing suit, sitting on a towel, shivering in the sun, with people about me chatting, and children running and splashing into the water, calling out to one another. Where was I? It took me several minutes to reorient myself, until I was no longer in Middle Earth but had made the long, long journey home. . . . "Someday," I told myself, "someday I'm going to

*Vietnamese orphans, some wrapped in blankets, sit on the floor of a World Airway DC8 jet at Yokata U.S. Air Force Base in Tokyo, on April 3, 1975. These South Vietnam refugees, as well as ones from Cambodia, would find many foster homes in the United States. Paterson's experiences with her foster children would inspire* The Great Gilly Hopkins.

write a book, and the central character is going to be a girl named Galadriel."[5]

Paterson's character's last name—Hopkins—arrived almost as quickly. Later, she recognized it as borrowed from Gerard Manley Hopkins, a favorite poet. In 1975, she possessed a name, not a story. Summer faded into fall, then winter, before the story finally developed.

Each year, Katherine Paterson wrote her church's holiday story. The tradition continued even after she became a successful novelist, with deadlines and obligations. Every year, she worried she would not be able to come up with a story. Yet every year, she did. That Christmas, she wrote about a kindly older man who takes in two unhappy and ungrateful foster children. She called it "Maggie's Gift," a title inspired by the title of O. Henry's 1906 story "The Gift of the Magi." Perhaps one of the best-known American short stories, it describes the Christmas preparations of Jim and Della Dillingham. To afford a watch chain for her husband's pocket watch, Della sells her hair. To buy his wife expensive combs for her long hair, Jim sells his watch. The conclusion, although sad, is meant to illustrate that true love is more valuable than any material possessions.

## THE GREAT GILLY HOPKINS

The New Year began with a new novel: *The Great Gilly Hopkins*. Gilly—Galadriel—was, in Paterson's words, "a foster child, born to a flower child who had read all of Tolkien but was still too much of child herself to care for a real live child of her own."[6] Shuffled from foster home to foster home—some kind, some cold, none a perfect fit—Gilly has given up. Her only dream is reuniting with the mother who abandoned her a dozen years before.

As the story begins, Gilly is moving into Maime Trotter's house. The overweight Bible-quoting Trotter has been raising William Earnest Teague, a shy and awkward seven-year-old boy. Her next-door neighbor, Mr. Randolph, is a regular dinner guest. Sent to guide a blind elderly man from his home, Gilly is upset when she realizes he is black. She has a similar bigoted response to her new teacher as well. Gilly sends her a racist poem anonymously, but Miss Harris recognizes the writing.

Miss Harris explains to Gilly, "Both of us are smart, and we know it. But the thing that brings us closer than intelligence is anger. You and I are two of the angriest people I know." Unlike Gilly, her teacher learned long ago to keep her anger bottled up. She thanks the girl for giving her an excuse to let that anger out; in fact, she explains that she spent 20 minutes in the teachers' lounge "cursing creatively."[7] Miss Harris lets Gilly leave without punishment, startling the girl, who on the way home does some creative cursing of her own. Gilly is equally cruel to her new foster mother, calling her fat, and her foster brother, calling him stupid.

Although Gilly is depicted as a mean, vulgar little girl, Paterson says one teacher actually complimented the author for creating a wonderful role model for today's youth. "Well, I don't know about you," Paterson remarked, "but I don't want for my children a role model who lies, steals, takes advantage of the handicapped, bullies the weak, acts out her racial bigotry in a particularly tasteless fashion, and regularly takes the Lord's name in vain."[8]

In creating a character like Gilly, Paterson is not championing the protagonist's choices, nor is she hoping readers emulate her. Instead, the author is depicting "a lost child who is angry with the world that regards her as disposable and who is fighting it with every available weapon fair or foul."[9]

Although shocked by the teacher who called Gilly a role model, Paterson was not surprised that many teachers and parents were upset at her "for bringing Gilly Hopkins into the world." Paterson likes Gilly just as she is and adds that

> if given a chance to reform her, I would flee in the opposite direction. Because children love Gilly. It seems that the worse they are, the more they love her. Which means, I believe with all my heart, that loving Gilly, they can begin a little to love themselves, and children who love themselves do not strike

out at other people. They do not shoot their classmates or blow up their schools. I would like children to take from a book I've written something that helps them love and value themselves.[10]

Perhaps the teacher who described Gilly as a role model noticed the drastic yet believable way she transforms. Loved unconditionally for the first time, Gilly eventually responds in kind. Near the end of the novel, Gilly's life at Trotter's is finally peaceful. It is an idealized "happy ending." In many similar books for young readers, that would be its conclusion. Instead, her earlier pleas for rescue from Trotter's home are finally heeded—not by her biological mother but by her grandmother. Enduring unexpected consequences to her actions, Gilly moves into the house where her mother once lived.

Her new stability is no happy ending. Nor is finally seeing her mother. The book's conclusion reflects *The Yearling*'s, a similarity the author recognized years after the book's publication. Calling Trotter from an airport, Gilly breathlessly sobs:

> "Trotter, it's all wrong. Nothing turned out the way it's supposed to."
>
> "How you mean supposed to? Life ain't supposed to be nothing, 'cept maybe tough."
>
> "But I always thought when my mother came. . ."
>
> "My sweet baby, ain't no one ever told you yet. I reckon I thought you had that all figured out."
>
> "What?"
>
> "That all that stuff about happy endings is lies. The only ending in this world is death. Now that might or might not be happy, but either way, you ain't ready to die, are you?"[11]

Paterson has wondered not only about *The Yearling*'s inspiration, but as someone raised by a mother and father who stayed married, she wonders,

> Why do I keep writing stories about children and young people who are orphaned or otherwise isolated and estranged? It's because I have within myself a lonely, frightened child who keeps demanding comfort. I have a rejected child, a jealous and jilted adolescent inside who demands, if not revenge, a certain degree of satisfaction. I am sure it is she, or should I say they, who keep demanding that I write for them.[12]

She wrote this novel not only for the scared child dwelling within her, but for scared children and teenagers who read her novels, touched by their honesty and unwillingness to embrace simplistic, unrealistic happy endings. In speeches about *Gilly*, she often quotes the young fan who hated to read until he read about Gilly. As he wrote in a letter to Paterson: "Thank you for the book, *The Great Gilly Hopkins*. I love the book. I am on page 16."[13]

*The Great Gilly Hopkins* earned the author a Newbery Honor medal, which is equivalent to an honorable mention. Considering the thousands of books competing for the award each year, it is a significant prize. The novel also earned a 1979 National Book Award. Established on March 16, 1950, this latter award began as one for adult literature, including poetry, fiction, and nonfiction. It soon included awards for children's literature, but every book is awarded a prize because it represents "the best of American literature" and because the work would "enhance the cultural value of good writing in America."[14]

Like *Terabithia*, *Gilly* was criticized for its language. Paterson recalls one adult offended by the profanity in *Terabithia* who told her that she would be better off with a biblical millstone around her neck than to continue to "write such books for the fragile young." Paterson adds, "Since I take the Bible very seriously, I did not laugh."[15] Despite such criticism, she quickly points out the librarian at a juvenile correctional facility that included "murderers and kids who

## Did you know...

The American Library Association (ALA) records challenges to books on the shelves of public and school libraries. The ALA Office for Intellectual Freedom defines a challenge "as a formal, written complaint, filed with a library or school requesting that materials be removed because of content or appropriateness. According to Judith F. Krug, director of the Office for Intellectual Freedom, the number of challenges reflects only incidents reported, and for each reported, four or five remain unreported."*

From 1990 to 2004, Katherine Paterson was on the top ten of the ALA's most frequently challenged authors. In 1991, for example, both Paterson's *Bridge to Terabithia* and *The Great Gilly Hopkins* appeared on the "Top 10 Challenged Books for 1991." The number one choice that year? Bret Easton Ellis's graphic, adult novel *American Psycho*.

* "The Most Frequently Challenged Books of 2007." American Library Association. http://www.ala.org/ala/aboutala/offices/oif/bannedbooksweek/challengedbanned/frequentlychallengedbooks.cfm#miofcb.

have committed violent crimes." The librarian sought out Paterson at a convention to tell her, "The other day a girl brought back a copy of *Gilly Hopkins* to the library. 'This is me,' she said." This, more than all the offended letters, truly affected the author, who confesses, "This is why I can't clean up my books. If a girl in a center for hardcore delinquents can identify with Gilly, then perhaps she can find someone who will be Trotter for her."[16]

Although the novel featured far less profanity than could be found in most television programs airing at 8:00 P.M., (once called the "family hour" by network programmers), some parents are still demanding that it be removed from school library shelves some 30 years after it was published. As often as a parent demands it be pulled from the library shelves for profanity, another wonders why a book with such a "bleak" ending is offered for young adults.

In response to such criticisms, Paterson, in a speech accepting the Regina Medal in 1988, described the stark differences between the Charles Dickens novel *Oliver Twist* and *Oliver!*, the musical based on his book. In the novel, young orphan Oliver escapes the punishment of the workhouse, is "employed" by master thief Fagin, and witnesses the murder of Nancy and then the death of her killer, Bill Sykes. Over three concluding chapters, Oliver and the other good characters are rewarded. The bad, like Fagin, are punished. Finally, a wealthy benefactor, Mr. Brownlow, takes the boy home. Most readers finish the novel content that all is well and Oliver will live happily ever after.

Not every musical is lighthearted and frivolous. Although *Oliver!* contained memorable songs and melodies, the director made a bold choice. In the film adaptation's conclusion, a carriage stops before Mr. Brownlow's estate. Brownlow and an exhausted Oliver disembark. The pair walks to the house, where the boy is hugged by Brownlow's housekeeper. There is no music, no words, and, as Paterson noted in her speech,

> his pain is not trivialized, much less erased. He will grow up to be a wise and compassionate gentleman, but deep in his heart, he will bear the hunger of the workhouse and the grief of Jacob's Island to his grave.
>
> This, I maintain, is a proper ending. Perhaps I should amend that. It is a proper ending for me. It is not, strictly speaking, a happy ending. It is certainly not happily ever after. But it is a positive demonstration of what I mean when I speak of hope in stories for children.[17]

*An illustration of the Taiping Rebellion, which occurred in China between 1850 and 1864. After completing* Jacob Have I Loved, *Paterson returned to historical fiction by setting her novel,* Rebels of the Heavenly Kingdom, *in this period of Chinese history.*

# 7

# First Person, Singular

KATHERINE PATERSON LAUGHS when she is asked if *Jacob Have I Loved* is the most autobiographical of her novels. For her, *Come Sing, Jimmy Jo* is far closer, but when pressed she says the main reason is, "I can't imagine I was that angry [when she was a child] but then I was very angry while I was writing [*Jacob*]."[1]

Set on Rass, a fictional island in Maryland's Chesapeake Bay, *Jacob Have I Loved* takes place during World War II, an era when the writer was the same age as main character, Sara Louise. While Paterson's rivalry was with her older sister, Elizabeth, Sara Louise's feelings of inadequacy are directed toward her twin, Caroline. Paterson discussed the feelings of unexpressed anger in a speech she gave about the novel:

> I know in my heart that the reason I nearly despaired of finishing [*Jacob Have I Loved*] was more the internal storms it stirred than those that came from without. I was trying to write a story that made my stomach churn every time I sat down at a typewriter. "Love is strong as death," says the writer of the Song of Songs, "jealousy is cruel as the grave." I did not want ever again to walk the dark path into the cruelty.[2]

Most of the characters depicted in novels are filtered through the experiences of the writer. In *On Writing*, Stephen King explains,

## Did you know...

The setting for *Jacob Have I Loved* was inspired by William Warner's *Beautiful Swimmers: Waterman, Crabs and the Chesapeake Bay*. Published in 1976, the book was a gift for Katherine Paterson's son John from her sister Helen. Reading it a few days after Christmas, the author knew she wanted to set her next novel in the area Warner's book described. His book would win a Pulitzer Prize in 1977, the year after James Michener's historical novel, *Chesapeake*, was published. Although Paterson worried about the well-known novelist covering the same region she was writing about, she quickly realized that they had radically different stories to tell.

I think you will find that, if you continue to write fiction, every character you create is partly you. When you ask yourself what a certain character will do given a certain set of circumstances, you're making the decision based on what you yourself would (or in the case of a bad guy, wouldn't) do.[3]

It does not matter if the story is set in a distant time or place, or if the protagonist is a different gender than the author. There is a connection to the creator. Writing about growing up, Paterson relies on memory as much as she does on observation. What made the novel *Jacob Have I Loved* distinct from her other works is the fact that the author wrote it in the first person.

This technique means the reader's point of view is that of the protagonist's. The main character narrates the events, and his or her version of the story is generally the only one the reader receives, such as this description offered by Sara Louise:

On Rass, sons represent wealth and security. What my mother bore [my father] were girls, twin girls. I was the elder by a few minutes. I always treasured the thought of those minutes. They represented the only time in my life when I was the center of everyone's attention. From the moment Caroline was born, she snatched it all for herself.[4]

Paterson later confessed, "I have always sworn that I would never write a book in the first person. It is too limiting, too egotistical. And yet, the book refused any voice but Louise's. 'Oh well,' I said to myself, 'I'd better get it down any way I can in the first draft. In the next draft I can write it properly.'"[5]

Nearly 30 years after its publication, many critics consider *Jacob Have I Loved* Paterson's most complex and literary work. Although fictional, its perspective and sharp (sometimes tragic) details recall adult memoirs, such as Mary Karr's *The Liars' Club*. When it was published, many reviewers recognized the depth of Paterson's latest work, like Betty Levin, who described *Jacob Have I Loved* as a "breathtaking novel ... full of humor and compassion and sharpness; it tells a story as old as myth and as fresh as invention."[6] Still, the novel earned some criticism. One reviewer asked:

> Must Peterson's capable, imaginative protagonist—the narrator in *Jacob Have I Loved*, Sara Louise Bradshaw, be forced in the name of historical accuracy, into the same kind of quietistic and blatantly anti-feminist womanhood as her mother before her? Why must we witness "Wheez" Bradshaw cheerfully trading her hopes of medical school for a marriage to a widowed farmer?[7]

In a speech, Paterson admitted she wanted to start "yelling at the critic." She also wondered, "What's this about her mother? What have you got against women who make the conscious choice to be homemakers? This woman had a fine husband who loved her. She raised two terrific daughters."[8]

## RETURN TO HISTORICAL FICTION

For half a dozen years, Paterson had concentrated on fiction that took place in the present, including *Bridge to Terabithia* and *The Great Gilly Hopkins*. *Jacob Have I Loved*, however, took place 40 years before its publication date but employed a modern, first-person-confessional technique. Yet despite their differences in subject matter and style, all three won major literary awards: *Jacob Have I Loved* earned the author her second Newbery Medal. Moving away from historical fiction had seemed risky, but by 1983, the author was ready for a 180-degree turn.

"From 1981 to the spring of 1983 I went about the country making speeches as I am tonight," Paterson explained to the listeners at the Simmons College Center for the study of Children's Literature. "Almost invariably during this timespan someone would say, 'I'm so glad you stopped writing historical novels.' And, of course, the person had no way of knowing that lying on my desk at that minute, waiting for me to return was the most ambitious historical novel I had ever attempted."[9]

For years, Paterson was asked why she never set one of her books in China, the country of her birth. In 1983, she finally did just that. Set during the nineteenth-century revolt by the Taiping Tienkuo against their Manchu rulers, *Rebels of the Heavenly Kingdom* was praised for its epic scale and historical accuracy, but a number of critics felt the characters were not very realistic and existed only to advance a moral point of view. "*Rebels*, I think it is safe to say, is my least-read book," the author admits. "A number of people have asked why I wrote it. The answer to that question is, simply, I had to write it. I could not help writing it."[10]

"Joseph Conrad once said that he never read his reviews, he measured them," Paterson noted, but negative reactions bothered the author regardless of their word count. After all, she explained, "I'm a reader, not a mathematician."[11] A writer can do little about bad reviews. They cannot "fix" later books because of what was said in reviews of earlier works. And altering novels to avoid criticism destroys both the story and the novel's integrity. Besides, trying to avoid criticism rarely eliminates unfavorable reviews.

## MOVING TO VERMONT

By the middle of the 1980s, John and Katherine Paterson moved once again. They relocated to a state that would inspire the author and radically alter her work. In 1986, they settled in Barre, Vermont. Their children were grown; they craved a change in scenery and a bit of adventure. Although closing in on an age when many retire, John Paterson began working as a minister in the quaint central Vermont town. His wife continued writing; novelists rarely retire.

Just south of state capital of Montpelier, Barre boasts the largest population in the area: around 9,000 residents. An idyllic-looking New England small town, it features a pavilion on the village green encircled by churches and small businesses. Downtown Barre is surrounded by the green mountains for which the state is named (after the description French explorer Samuel de Champlain gave to the area: "verde mont," or "green mountains.")

Soon after the Patersons' move, the Vermont Migrant Education Project contacted the author. Compiling data on the percentages of students who drop out of high school, state officials learned the children of migrant dairy workers dropped out more than any other group. The reasons seemed obvious. Migrant workers moved often. Their children faced an interrupted education and isolation from their peers. They had trouble keeping up with their grade level. Frustrated, many of them abandoned school as soon as they were able.

The Migrant Education Project pursued a solution: Vermont authors and illustrators would be enlisted to create books that were easy to read and reflected the children's circumstances. The children of migrant workers would receive copies of their own during special summer programs; in the fall the books would appear in the schools they attended.

Hopefully, having become familiar with a book new to the other students, the children would feel they had a leg up.

"Now I have never been one to believe you should write books to address problems—or even a narrow audience," Paterson later explained.

> It has been my experience that the book you think is perfect to help a particular child with a special problem is not the book the actual child would choose at all. But when I was asked "as a Vermont writer" to contribute to the program, I'd only lived in the state a few weeks and I was so flattered to be called "a Vermont writer" that I joyfully accepted the challenge.[12]

Before embarking on the project, illustrators and authors were sent to dairy farms so they could understand the conditions children of migrant workers grew up in. Although she had not grown up on a farm, Paterson had an advantage. She had moved 18 times before her eighteenth birthday and deeply understood what it was like to feel isolated and alone.

*The Smallest Cow in the World* was published by the Vermont Migrant Education Project in 1988; three years later it was republished by HarperCollins. Created for children younger than her usual audience, the book was simple, funny, and real. Some aspects of the book even mirrored *The Yearling*. Instead of a deer, the protagonist, Marvin, loves and loses a cow. Replaced by an imaginary cow—the smallest cow in the title—Marvin's sister May explained, "No matter how small she is or where she lives or if she's smart or dumb, Rosie will have Dad and Mom and you and me and the smallest calf in the world. She will never be lonely again."[13]

The book not only attracted an audience beyond the original small group for which it was written, it also gained an unexpected fan: Katherine Paterson. Although the author generally avoids sequels, she has now written two additional books about Marvin: *Marvin's Best Christmas Present Ever* and *Marvin One Too Many*, the latter's title reflecting both the author's mixed feelings about sequels and the storyline itself.

Besides writing for a younger audience, Paterson continued to write young-adult novels like 1985's *Come Sing, Jimmy Jo*. The novel is told through the eyes of a poor Appalachian boy who becomes a successful country singer. Paterson explained on her Web site:

> I wrote "Come Sing, Jimmy Jo," while I was still struggling with the dilemma a very private person (who is also a show-off) meets when she is suddenly "famous." I loved parts of being famous (being, as I say, a natural born show-off) but I hated the parts of it that seemed to invade my private spaces.[14]

*Park's Quest*, published in 1988, follows the title character as he learns about his father, who was killed in Vietnam. *The St. James Guide to Children's Writers* notes that in *Park's Quest*,

> allusion and imagery specifically connect Park's quest with those of Parzival and the Arthurian knights' search for the Holy Grail. Thus *Park's Quest*, like *Jacob Have I Loved* (1980), emphasizes the mythological and metaphysical dimensions that make each so much more than realistic problem novels. *Jacob Have I Loved* explores within a family setting the mystery of God's love, coexistent with a kind of impersonality, a love that breaks through even self-inflicted blinders. Initiated and enlightened through their trials, both Park Broughton and Louise Bradshaw become like the merciful father: through them compassion and healing flow out to others.[15]

Paterson's work on *The Smallest Cow in the World* allowed the author to learn about her state. In the 1990s, she began writing novels inspired by her new home's history. It was a history as inspiring and as tragic as any in her modern novels.

*Dairy farmers bring milk to a Vermont cheese factory in this circa 1870s illustration. After moving to Vermont in the 1980s, Paterson discovered that the state's history and people would inspire a number of her novels.*

# 8

# Organizing

IN THE SECOND-FLOOR office of her nineteenth-century farmhouse, Katherine Paterson had spent several years writing books for children, including *The Tale of the Mandarin Ducks* and *The Smallest Cow in the World*. During that time, she was also brushing up on the history of her new home. Barre, home to the Vermont History Center, was an ideal place for the author to conduct her research. There, Paterson researched the historical novels she would soon set in Vermont. She learned about the lives lived by young people in the nineteenth century, a time when many people worked long hours in dangerous jobs.

She quickly realized that although Vermont was a tiny state, it was overflowing with stories.

With just 600,000 residents, Vermont is one of the least populous states in the country. According to the U.S. Census, it is also 95 percent white. Despite this seeming lack of diversity, it is by no means homogenous, a word defined by Webster's Online Dictionary as "of the same or a similar kind or nature."[1]

Vermont is instead defined by the distinct contrasts among its citizens. While native Vermont farmers till the soil and raise animals, as they have for centuries, the state's numerous ski areas attract tourists from around the world. Beside ramshackle farmhouses are rebuilt homes like the Patersons', which are owned by "flatlanders." These transplants from cities in nearby states like Connecticut, Massachusetts, and New York often find themselves in conflict with natives who are sometimes poor and often politically conservative. In addition to the natives and transplants, pockets of communes remain nearly 40 years after the hippie ideals of the 1960s have faded.

This dichotomy between rich and poor, native and outsider provided fertile ground for a writer seeking conflict in her fiction. Today, Paterson admits that friction has ebbed somewhat, joking that it is partly because so many people have moved into Vermont that "the flatlanders won."[2] As a well-traveled novelist, Paterson has something in common with cosmopolitan neighbors from urban areas. Yet, because she grew up and spent much of her adulthood in rural areas, the author understands Vermont's natives as well.

## WRITING AND SOCIAL JUSTICE

In 1991, Paterson was a participant in the Women's History Project celebrating Vermont's bicentennial. That work led to *Lyddie*, her first Vermont young-adult novel set over 150 years ago. Beginning in 1843, the story opens with 12-year-old Lyddie being "sold" to an inn to pay her father's debts. Inspired by the well-dressed "factory girls" who visit, she makes her way to Lowell, Massachusetts, to become one herself. There she endures 13-hour days and miserable conditions for low wages.

As a native Vermonter, Lyddie's speech and dress are radically different from most of the women she meets who live in Massachusetts. The conflicts created by those who judge and disparage Lyddie allowed Paterson to reflect on class differences and snobbery. Yet the backdrop of a grim textile mill presented a chance to comment on even larger issues.

Fiction can be more than an escape. Characters in novels and the challenges they face allow authors opportunities to express points of view about political and social situations and injustices. "If the novel were not one of the most important factors of modern life, . . . if its influence were not greater than all the pulpits, than all the newspapers between the oceans, it would not be so important that its message should be true,"[3] wrote author Frank Norris in a 1902 essay, "The Responsibilities of the Novelist," as quoted by Maura Spiegel.

One example of a novel that had a huge impact on society is Harriet Beecher Stowe's *Uncle Tom's Cabin*. The book was a best seller, selling 10,000 copies in its first week and 300,000 the year it was published. Yet the 1852 novel was more than a popular book. Its antislavery theme and graphic description of life as a slave influenced readers to support the abolitionist cause. The novel is often credited as a factor in helping to spark the American Civil War (1861–1865), during which most slaves in the United

States were freed. (Slaves were freed in the rebel states in 1863 by the Emancipation Proclamation; the rest were freed shortly after the war when slavery was abolished by the Thirteenth Amendment to the U.S. Constitution.) Indeed, President Abraham Lincoln supposedly remarked upon meeting Stowe, "So *you're* the little woman who wrote the book that started this great war!"[4]

Other novels that tackled social issues would follow. In 1906, Upton Sinclair's novel *The Jungle* exposed the filth and misery endured by an immigrant working in Packingtown, Chicago's meat-packing "village." Although Sinclair wrote the novel in part to highlight the area's grim working environment, it was instead the disgusting conditions surrounding meat and other food preparation that outraged readers. As a result of the novel's influence, President Theodore Roosevelt demanded an investigation that led to Congress passing the Pure Food and Drug Act of 1906.

Although written about a time long past, *Lyddie* and the novel that followed, *Jip*, highlight not only the harsh conditions of their times, but also issues that affect people in the early twenty-first century. In the 1840s, women were not allowed to vote. When they married, their property became that of their husbands'. Lyddie's story is the story of a girl who achieves independence despite enormous obstacles. Yet it is also the story of her fellow female textile workers who organized and fought for better wages and working conditions decades before better-known, male-led labor actions transpired.

Authors whose fiction addresses social issues face greater risks than novelists who aspire only to entertain. Readers who do not share an author's worldview might be alienated, and many feel that moralizing books designed more to alter public opinion than to tell a good story are often boring. The larger a writer's audience, the greater the risk: A popular author like Paterson faces losing thousands of fans. Although few modern readers support 13-hour days or the unsafe workplaces depicted in *Lyddie*, twenty-first-century Americans disagree about work-related issues. Pro-union voices contrast with those who view these organizations as harmful to the economy. As a Presbyterian, Paterson sees Judeo-Christian beliefs and social justice as going hand-in hand: "Helping the poor is in the scriptures."[5]

Paterson was inspired to write *Lyddie* because she remembers studying history in school, when it seemed like nothing but one war after another. The stories of lives lived between wars and the lives of the poor who struggled were rarely told. Even less so were depictions of younger people, many not yet teenagers, who were worked mercilessly on the factories and farms of the 1800s.

*Lyddie*'s conclusion stands out against the ending of *Jacob Have I Loved*. Although the novelist did not write *Lyddie* to answer critics, this novel's protagonist made a radically different choice than the one made by *Jacob*'s Sara Louise. Lyddie comes of age at a time when women were expected to marry young. Factory life was a short one because those who stayed in it too long often became very sick. Luke Stevens, who falls for Lyddie, is a kindhearted Quaker, the kind of man many women of the era would have seen as the perfect husband. Yet Lyddie rejects his proposal. She does not want to be supported, nor does she want to give up her independence. She does not even want to return to the farm she grew up on, a property he now owns:

"Then if thee will not stay, where will thee go?" Luke asked Lyddie.

She stopped in the middle of the road, her whole body alight with the thrill of it. "I'm off," she said, "to Ohio. There is a college there that will take a woman just like a man."[6]

## JIP

When she finished writing *Lyddie*, Paterson found herself convinced that there were more stories to tell about life in the middle of the nineteenth century. And she was right. While Lyddie's journey was an escape from farm to mill life, the journey taken by the protagonist in *Jip* would take readers back to the farm.

Researching the history of Vermont poorhouses, Paterson discovered the true story of Putnam Proctor Wilson, who was placed in a wooden cage, along with others considered insane, in a property adjacent to Hartford, Vermont's poorhouse in the early 1800s. "These men were raving crazy most of the time," an eyewitness account noted, "and there caged up in narrow, filthy cages . . . the inhuman treatment to which they were subjected was sufficient of itself to make lunatics of all men. Poor old Putnam had some rational moments and was always pleased to see children to whom he would sing."[7]

The image of a filthy man in a wooden cage who, despite his imprisonment sang to children inspired the author to write *Jip*, a 1996 novel that commented on society's response to the poor and mentally ill as strongly as *Lyddie* had on labor. In crafting the fictional story of Jip, Paterson used a character based on the real-life Putnam to inspire the protagonist's own quest for freedom.

Set a decade after *Lyddie*, the story in *Jip* unfolds on a Vermont poor farm. In the 1800s, just as today, how communities deal with transients, the poor, and severe mental illness was a source of ongoing debate. In the novel,

Jip remembers how Otis Lyman, the farm's manager, explained it:

> In the good old days, as Mr. Lyman often reminded them, the able-bodied of the poor would have been let out to the highest bidder and would have brought a good bit of money to the town instead of draining the town purse. But some do-gooders claimed this practice smacked too close to southern slavery, so they began to put out the poor to the lowest bidder—the householder who proposed to take on the responsibility for the pauper at the least expense to the town. This practice, alas, fell into disfavor as the ever vigilant do-gooders sniffed out cases of abuse and claimed near-starvation. So out of Christian charity the town had purchased for their benefit—*for their benefit*—this wonderful farm and hired the Lymans to manage it and the lives of all those unfortunate paupers for whom the town must be responsible.[8]

The farm took in those who could not pay their debts, transients regularly swept from the village and into the poor house, and the mentally ill. For the latter group, this solution was cheaper than paying for their upkeep at the mental institution in nearby Brattleboro. At the beginning of the book, Jip is hired to build a cage to keep the man he will befriend and who will also help Jip escape the prison of the poor house.

### END OF THE CENTURY

Katherine Paterson's next novel, *Preacher's Boy*, was set at the end of the nineteenth century, a period often referred to as the *fin de siècle*, a French term meaning the "end of the century." It was a time of excitement and concern, of endings and beginnings, much like the end of the twentieth century would later be. "It's my little joke that while everyone in the world right now is looking forward, I'm looking back,"[9] the author commented in a 1999 interview.

Through this story of a rambunctious son of a preacher who wants to break from organized religion, Paterson had the opportunity to explore the challenges that come with being the child of a minister. "Writing about people who are good can be a real challenge," she admitted. "I was especially interested in the character of the [minister] father because so many books have fathers who are physically or emotionally absent. I know lots of good fathers, some in my own family, and I was very determined to write about a father who was trying to do the best by his children."[10]

*Preacher's Boy* also helped Paterson to look at the many ways new technologies retool society. She recalled, "It was sometime around 1900 that someone said everything's that going to be invented has been invented. We can laugh at that now, but, of course, society was utterly changed by all the new technology."[11]

In order to understand the late-nineteenth-century changes Paterson described in her novel, it is important to note that they had their start more than a century prior. The Industrial Revolution brought about radical changes when it began in the mid-eighteenth century. In Britain, for example, skilled workers were assisted by precision machines, while in the United States, unskilled workers from rural areas moved to factory towns, where they essentially became part of the machines they labored on.

People's lives were reshaped by the inventions of the Industrial Revolution. British inventor James Watt's development of the steam engine or Eli Whitney's creation of interchangeable parts are but two examples of inventions that forever altered the way people lived, traveled, and worked. "The term 'Yankee ingenuity' could have been coined with Whitney in mind," writer Curt Anderson claims. "Americans solved issues of speed and mass production. In 1798, American Eli Whitney secured a US government contract (for $134,000) to produce 10,000 army muskets. Whitney refined and successfully applied the 'Uniformity-System' of production using inter-changeable parts." Although first met with skepticism, Whitney succeeded by

> convincingly demonstrating to President John Adams the workability of the inter-changeable parts concept. He showed Adams that randomly selected parts would fit together as a whole working musket. Whitney then single-handedly designed and built all the machinery to produce the weapons ... all before a solitary worker entered the factory. Later, in 1818, Whitney invented the first milling machine.[12]

Beginning with Whitney's interchangeable parts, which made mass production possible, to the advances that enabled textile workers to produce more in less time, the advances of the 1800s radically altered the average worker's life. Such workers traded small towns and family farms for big cities and impersonal factories. Faced with difficult, even dangerous conditions, they often banded together in collective bargaining associations later called unions.

### BREAD AND ROSES, TOO

The labor actions of the early twentieth century would help inform Paterson's next historical novel, *Bread and Roses, Too*, which was published in 2006.

This novel was based on true events from the early 1900s. At the Socialist Labor Hall in Barre, Paterson became fascinated by an old black-and-white photo of children. They were refugees sheltered by Barre residents in 1912. They were not, however, escapees from a war or foreign citizens fleeing a government collapse. They were the offspring of adults engaged in a brutal labor strike just to the south in Massachusetts.

Like the struggles in *Lyddie*, the conflict in *Bread and Roses, Too* focused on labor issues in a Massachusetts mill town. *Lyddie*, set in the 1840s, took place before much of the modernization created by the Industrial Revolution. Set in 1912, *Bread and Roses, Too* demonstrated how worker's lives had scarcely improved 70 years later. The differences between those times were, in fact, relatively minor: Immigrants from Ireland who would work for less pay were

## *Did you know...*

The inspiration for *Bread and Roses, Too* was a real life strike in Lawrence, Massachusetts. After one mill owner's wage reduction for his workers, laborers went on strike, a labor action that soon involved more than 20,000 workers at nearly every textile mill in the town. Prompted by a state law that reduced the maximum hours a worker could labor from 56 to 54, the owners reduced weekly pay. The strike was significant because few believed that the predominately immigrant, uneducated women would stick together. They did; the strike lasted over two months. While the strike caused mill owners to increase wages, the concessions disappeared within the year. However, the strike inspired many more such labor movements.

supplanting young Lyddie and other workers at her textile mill; by 1912, Italian immigrants were proving even cheaper to pay. But the newcomers in both novels were being taken advantage of.

By taking the viewpoints of Rosa, a daughter of a striking worker, and Jake, a petty thief the same age as Rosa, Paterson offered a way for readers to see how poor people felt. Rosa is skeptical because she is experiencing the events as someone uprooted by them. Jake, however, is more of a witness to the triumph and tragedy. By employing two alternating lead characters, Paterson gives the reader a more fully evolved narrative.

The book's publication was greeted with near universal acclaim. "Paterson has skillfully woven true events and real historical figures into the fictional story and created vivid settings, clearly drawn characters, and a strong sense of the hardship and injustice faced by mostly immigrant mill workers," noted a critic for *School Library Journal*. "Ethnic rivalries and prejudices play an important role, and the alternating viewpoints of Rosa and Jake allow for a broader picture and add tension and balance."[13]

*The movie poster of* Bridge to Terabithia, *the 2007 film directed by Gabor Csupo and cowritten by Paterson's son David, whose childhood experiences inspired the original novel.*

# 9

# Making Movies

FOR BARRE RESIDENTS, October 7, 2006, was a special day honoring their town's hospitality to immigrants nearly a century before. For Katherine Paterson the honor was more personal; her novel *Bread and Roses, Too* had just been published, and posters advertising the event described her as a "local author." Along with a chance to meet Paterson, the Saturday-afternoon celebration included an historical reenactment sponsored by the Aldrich Public Library and the Barre Historical Society, a parade, and a speech on mill conditions in Lawrence, Massachusetts.

By then, Paterson was regularly introduced as a "Vermont writer," a description she appreciates. She is not only happy in her adoptive state, she has found a treasure trove of material. More of her novels are at least partly set in Vermont than anywhere else.

After a lifetime of travel, author Paterson has settled into life in the small Vermont town. She is active with her church, the Author's Guild, and the Children's Book Guild of Washington, D.C. She continues to lecture and visits local schools regularly. In 1995, John Paterson retired from the ministry, but he continues to assist his wife as her first editor.

## FROM PAGE TO SCREEN

In early 2007, Katherine Paterson celebrated another milestone. Although *Bridge to Terabithia* had already been produced as a play and a one-hour TV movie, that year it was released as a full-length feature film. The movie's premiere was the culmination of a long journey, not only for the author, but for her son as well. As previously mentioned, the novel had been incredibly personal for the writer because it had been inspired by the death of her son's friend. Some 30 years after Lisa Hill's death, David Paterson turned his mother's novel into a screenplay.

As a young adult, David Paterson pursued a career in the arts working as both an actor and a playwright. In his spare time, he volunteered as a firefighter with the Manhasset Fire Department in New York. On September 11, 2001, he assisted in the rescue efforts after the terrorist attack on the World Trade Center's Twin Towers. Among the nearly 3,000 killed from the attacks, 343 firefighters and paramedics lost their lives.

*David and Katherine Paterson attend the premiere of* Bridge *to* Terabithia *at the El Capitan Theater in Hollywood, California, on February 3, 2007. Both mother and son were very pleased with the final film.*

As an eyewitness to so much death, David Paterson found himself returning to the first loss that truly touched him, as well as his mother's literary response. *Bridge to Terabithia* was a novel he had long resisted reading. "David still, now with two boys of his own, finds *Bridge* a very difficult book to read," his mother explained on her Web site. "It is too close to the bone. Any therapeutic value the book had was for me, facing not only Lisa's death but my own mortality call."[1]

When David Paterson asked his mother for permission to turn *Bridge to Terabithia* into a screenplay, she agreed. When a successful parent offers their offspring a leg up in their own profession it can seem like nepotism—favoritism based on the family connection. Yet this time it made sense. His suffering, as well as his mother's, had inspired the work. Katherine Paterson trusts her son but perhaps more importantly considers him a talented writer. Yet even his mother's blessing was no guarantee the movie would be made.

The transition from book to film took time. No matter their connections, every first-time screenwriter confronts tremendous challenges. Thousands of scripts compete for limited production money. Although having the right to produce a script from a successful novel made David Paterson's work easier, it was hardly easy. In an interview, he noted, "If you can believe this, I did meet with some companies that asked if I could just 'hurt' Leslie a little bit, put her in a light coma and then bring her out."[2]

Few writers have much of a say when a movie is made from their novel. The author of the Harry Potter novels, J.K. Rowling, was able to exercise control not only on the script, but also on casting and director approval. It is far more common that novelists will not even know how radically their books have been changed until they see the films at the premieres.

On the DVD commentary, Katherine Paterson says she is pleased with the movie and grateful the special effects did not overwhelm the story. In an interview, the author succinctly points out one big reason for the lack of special effects: "the budget was too low."[3]

Although the lack of money for special effects was a factor, the key reason the filmmakers were able to make it clear that the land of "Terabithia" was a figment of Jesse and Leslie's imagination was due to David Paterson's script. Although coproduced by Walden Media (along with the Walt Disney Studios), the same company that produced *The Lion, the Witch and the Wardrobe*, Terabithia was clearly not Narnia, where an entire other world exists on the other side of the wardrobe.

## THE WRITING CONTINUES

While Katherine Paterson enjoys seeing her novels turned into movies, she is a writer at heart. For over 40 years she

*Did you know...*

In April 2008, Killer Films signed Katherine Paterson and her son David's production company, Arcady Bay Entertainment, to a three-picture development deal. Their first project? *The Great Gilly Hopkins*, with a script written by David and a film budget of $8 million to $10 million. "The opportunity to have a prize-winning, beloved novel and the chance to do what we do with that kind of raw material is exciting," Killer Films cofounder and copresident told entertainment industry newspaper *Variety*. "David's adaptation kept hold of what's beautiful and timeless about the book."*

---

* Winter Miller, "Killer Films Pacts with Arcady Bay." *Variety*. http://www.variety.com/article/VR1117984816.html?categoryid=1238&cs=1.

has written books for young people, and most of them begin the same way: with a pen and paper. Author Natalie Goldberg explains the value of this:

> Writing is physical and is affected by the equipment you use. In typing, your fingers hit the keys and the result is block, black letters: a different aspect of yourself may come out. I have found that when I am writing something emotional, I must write it the first time directly with hand on paper. Handwriting is more connected to the movement of the heart.[4]

Considering the emotional quality of her work, it is not surprising that Paterson prefers to start her stories by hand. Unfortunately, the decades of writing in longhand have exacted a physical toll. "Dickens and Austen wrote by hand," the author laments, "and I don't remember them getting carpal tunnel."[5] Charles Dickens and Jane Austen wrote in a time before typewriters or computers; Paterson's output is at least competitive with Dickens's.

Now in her seventies, she has surrendered only slightly to time's passage. Besides forcing herself to type her first drafts, she and her husband have moved their bedroom to the first floor because the couple's children worry about them regularly negotiating the farmhouse's stairs. Still, Paterson continues to create in the early mornings from her second-floor office, "before my inner critic is awake,"[6] she jokes. In 2009, the author completed *The Day of the Pelican*, a modern-day novel in which the young protagonist and her family are refugees from the war in Kosovo and seek refuge in Vermont. The events of 9/11 bring more challenges for this Muslim family, but the United States is their home now, and they cannot return to their native land.

Katherine Paterson realizes some of her readers may dream of becoming professional writers and explains, "The world is full of people with talent; but the world is not full of people with persistence. If you have both talent and persistence, then you will probably succeed."[7]

Paterson herself has succeeded beyond her wildest dreams—certainly more than the girl who dreamed of becoming a missionary or a movie star. While humble about her talents, she is effusive about the value of her gifts. "I'm very biblically orientated, and so for me the most important thing is for the word to become flesh," she told the audience at the 2000 Children's Literature Festival. "I can write stories for children, and in that sense I can offer them words, but [teachers] are the word become flesh. . . . Society has taught our children that they are nobodies unless their faces appear on television.

"I want to say to that isolated, angry, fearful child . . . 'You are not alone, you are not despised, you are unique and of infinite value in the human family.'"[8] This is a value found every day, in the novels of Katherine Paterson.

# CHRONOLOGY

**1932**    Katherine Anne Clements Womeldorf is born on Halloween (October 31) in Huaiyin (formerly Qingjiang), China, to George and Mary Elizabeth.

**1937**    She relocates with her family (except for her father) to Richmond, Virginia.

**1938–1939**    She returns to China, living primarily in Shanghai while her father continues teaching in Huaiyin.

**1940**    She returns to the United States, where her father works as a minister in Winston-Salem, North Carolina.

**1950**    After attending 18 schools in 18 years, she graduates from Charles Town High School in Charles Town, Virginia.

**1950–1954**    She attends King College in Bristol, Tennessee and graduates summa cum laude with an A.B. degree in 1954.

**1954–1955**    She works as a sixth-grade teacher at Lovettsville Elementary School in Virginia.

**1955–1957**    She attends the Presbyterian School of Christian Education in Richmond, Virginia and earns an M.A. degree in Christian education in 1957.

**1957–1959**    She attends the Naganuma School of Japanese Language in Japan.

**1957–1961**    She works as a missionary at the Presbyterian Church Board of World Missions in Shikoku Island, Japan.

**1961–1962**    She attends the Union Theological Seminary in New York and earns her M.R.E., her second master's degree, in 1962. She marries John Barstow Paterson on July 14, 1962.

**1962–1963**    She works as a substitute teacher in New York.

**1963–1965**    She works as master of sacred studies and English at the Pennington School for Boys in New Jersey.

**1964**    Paterson has her first job as a professional writer, writing Sunday-school-curriculum guides for the Presbyterian Church.

**1965** Her son, John Barstow Paterson Jr., is born; she and her husband adopt Elizabeth Po Lin.

**1966** The Paterson family settles in Tacoma Park, Maryland; they adopt a second daughter, Mary Katherine Nahhesahpechea, who was born on an Apache reservation; Paterson's first book, a religious-education volume titled *Who Am I?*, is published; their second son, David Lord Paterson, is born.

**1968** She begins taking an adult education class on creative writing and starts work on a novel.

**1973** Her first novel, *The Sign of the Chrysanthemum*, is published.

**1974** David's best friend, Lisa Hill, is killed; Katherine Paterson begins to write the novel that will become *Bridge to Terabithia*.

**1977** *The Master Puppeteer* wins a National Book Award for Children's Literature; the family moves to Norfolk, Virginia; *Bridge to Terabithia* is published.

**1978** *Bridge to Terabithia* wins a Newbery Medal; *The Great Gilly Hopkins*, inspired by Paterson's experiences as a foster parent, is published.

**1979** *The Great Gilly Hopkins* is a Newbery Medal Honor Book; Paterson wins a National Book Award for Children's Literature.

**1981** *Jacob Have I Loved* wins a Newbery Medal.

**1986** John and Katherine Paterson relocate to Barre, Vermont.

**1991** *Lyddie*, the first of Paterson's nineteenth-century novels set in Vermont, is published.

**2007** *Bridge to Terabithia*, with a screenplay cowritten by David Paterson, is released as a feature film.

**2008** *The Great Gilly Hopkins* is developed as a movie.

**2009** *The Day of the Pelican* is published.

# NOTES

## Chapter 1

1 Katherine Paterson, *The Invisible Child: On Reading and Writing for Children*. New York: Dutton Children's Books, 2001, p. 255.

2 Ibid.

3 Katherine Paterson, foreword to *Part of Me Died, Too: Stories of Creative Survival Among Bereaved Children and Teenagers*, by Virginia Lynn Fry. Dutton Children's Books: New York, 1995, p. xii.

4 Paterson, *The Invisible Child*, pp. 253–254.

5 Peter T. Chattaway, "Deeper into Terabithia: *Bridge to Terabithia* Author Katherine Paterson Says a Story Reveals a Writer's Faith, Whether She Likes It or Not." *Christianity Today*, March 2007, p. 64.

## Chapter 2

1 Paterson, *The Invisible Child*, pp. 131–132.

2 Ibid., p. 132.

3 Ibid., p. 131.

4 Ibid., p. 203.

5 Katherine Paterson, telephone interview with John Bankston, October 5, 2008.

6 Paterson, *The Invisible Child*, p. 211.

7 Ibid., p. 155.

8 Hallett Abend, "New Era in China Held Very Fragile," *New York Times*, September 17, 1928, p. 10.

9 Ibid.

10 Hallett Abend, "Chinese Reds Gain, Kuomintang Losing," *New York Times*, January 21, 1932, p. 11.

11 Susan Townsend, "Japan's Quest for Empire 1931–1945," BBC. http://www.bbc.co.uk/history/worldwars/wwtwo/japan_quest_empire_04.shtml.

12 Katherine Paterson, *Gates of Excellence: On Reading and Writing Books for Children*. New York: Dutton Children's Books, 1981, as quoted in *Contemporary Authors Online*, Gale, 2008. Reproduced in *Biography Resource Center*. Farmington Hills, Mich.: Gale, 2008.

13 Paterson, interview.

14 Paterson, *Gates of Excellence*.

15 Paterson, *The Invisible Child*, p. 27.

16 Paterson, *Gates of Excellence*.

17 Katherine Paterson, "About Katherine Paterson," Penguin Group USA. http://us.penguingroup.com/nf/Author/AuthorPage/0,,1000024957,00.html.

18 Paterson, *Gates of Excellence*.

19 Paterson, interview.

20 Paterson, *The Invisible Child*, p. 65.

21 Ibid., p. 151.

22 Paterson, "About Katherine Paterson."

23 Katherine Paterson as quoted in *Contemporary Authors Online*, Gale, 2008. Reproduced in *Biography Resource Center*. Farmington Hills, Mich.: Gale, 2008.

24 Paterson, *The Invisible Child*, p. 32.

25 Virginia Buckley, "Katherine Paterson," *Horn Book*, August 1978, p. 370.

26 Paterson, "About Katherine Paterson."

27 Paterson, interview.

28 Paterson, "About Katherine Paterson."

29 Natalie Goldberg, *Writing Down the Bones: Freeing the Writer Within*. Boston: Shambhala Publications, 1986, p. 79.

30 Paterson, *Gates of Excellence*.

31 Paterson, "About Katherine Paterson."

## Chapter 3

1 Paterson, *Gates of Excellence*.

2 Paterson, interview.

3 Anne Lamott, *Bird by Bird: Some Instructions on Writing and Life*. New York: Pantheon Books, 1994, pp. 21–22.

4 Paterson, interview.

5 Paterson, "About Katherine Paterson."

6 Paterson, *The Invisible Child*, p. 251.

7 Ibid., p. 203.

8 Ibid., p. 251.

9 Paterson, interview.

10 Paterson, "About Katherine Paterson."

11 Paterson, interview.

12 Paterson, "About Katherine Paterson."

13 Ibid.

14 Paterson, *The Invisible Child*, p. 220.

15 Paterson, "About Katherine Paterson."

16 Stephen King, *On Writing: A Memoir of the Craft*. New York: Pocket Books, 2000, pp. 158–159.

17 Paterson, "About Katherine Paterson."

18 Paterson, *The Invisible Child*, p. xi.

19 Ibid.

20 Paterson, "About Katherine Paterson."

## Chapter 4

1 Paterson, *The Invisible Child*, p. 114.

2 Paterson, *The Invisible Child*, p. 251.

3 Lamott, *Bird by Bird*, p. xxiii.

4 Paterson, interview.

5 Ibid.

6 Ibid.

7 Virginia Haviland, as quoted on back flap of *Nightingales that Weep* and on "Katherine Paterson," *Authors and Artists for Young Adults*, Volume 31. Gale Group, 2000. Reproduced in *Biography Resource Center*. Farmington Hills, Mich.: Gale, 2008.

8 Paterson, *The Invisible Child*, p. 155.

9 Ibid., p. 146.

10 Alice Pope, ed., *2009 Children's Writer's & Illustrator's Market*. Cincinnati, Oh.: Writer's Digest Books, 2008, p. 186.

## Chapter 5

1 Paterson, *The Invisible Child*, p. 246.

2 Ibid., pp. 246–247.

3 Ibid., p. 247.

4 Ibid., pp. 247–248.

5 Katherine Paterson, "These Are Questions Recently Asked by Children and Educators in an Internet Interview with Katherine Paterson." Terabithia.com. http://www.terabithia.com/questions.html.

6 Paterson, *The Invisible Child*, p. 248.

7 Ibid.

8 Ibid., p. 249.

9 Katherine Paterson, *Bridge to Terabithia*. New York: HarperCollins Children's Books, 1977, p. 126.

10 Jack Forman, "Review of *Bridge to Terabithia*," *School Library Journal*, November 1977, p. 61.

11 Joan Oleck, "*Bridge to Terabithia* Hits the Big Screen: Author Katherine Paterson's Son Writes Screenplay to Newbery-winning Novel," *School Library Journal*, February 2007, p. 20.

12 Paterson, *The Invisible Child*, p. 246.

13 Katherine Paterson, "The Responsibility to Write: Stay True to Your Heart and Mind, Not the Latest Fad. (Off the Cuff)." *Writer*, March 2003, p. 20.

14 "The John Newbery Medal," American Library Association. http://www.ala.org/ala/mgrps/divs/alsc/awardsgrants/bookmedia/newberymedal/aboutnewbery/aboutnewbery.cfm.

15 Paterson, *Bridge to Terabithia*, dedication page.

16 Paterson, *The Invisible Child*, p. 250.

## Chapter 6

1 "Last Chopper out of Saigon," *Time*, May 12, 1975. http://www.time.com/time/magazine/article/0,9171,917411-1,00.html.

2 Paterson, *The Invisible Child*, p. 185.

3 Ibid., pp. 185–186.

4 Ibid., p. 186.

5 Ibid., p. 187.

6 Ibid., p. 188.

7 Katherine Paterson, *The Great Gilly Hopkins*, New York: HarperCollins, 1978, pp. 58–59.

8 Paterson, *The Invisible Child*, p. 190.

9 Ibid., p. 191.

10 Ibid., p. 32.

11 Paterson, *The Great Gilly Hopkins*, New York: HarperCollins, 1978, p. 147.

12 Katherine Paterson, "The Aim of the Writer Who Writes for Children," *Theory into Practice*, Autumn 1982, pp. 325–331.

13 Paterson, *The Invisible Child*, p. 241.

14 "About Us—History of the National Book Foundation," National Book Foundation. http://www.nationalbook.org/aboutus_history.html.

15 Katherine Paterson, "Why Do You Write for Children," *Theology Today*, January 2000, reproduced in *U.S. Catholic*, April 2001, Humanities Module, p. 28.

16 Ibid.

17 Paterson, *The Invisible Child*, p. 143.

## Chapter 7

1 Paterson, interview.

2 Paterson, *The Invisible Child*, pp. 214–215.

3 King, *On Writing*, p. 191.

4 Katherine Paterson, *Jacob Have I Loved*. New York: HarperCollins, 1980, p. 18.

5 Paterson, *The Invisible Child*, p. 215.

6 Betty Levin, "A Funny, Sad, Sharp Look Back at Growing Up," *Christian Science Monitor*, January 21, 1981, p. 17.

7 James Holt McGavran Jr., "Bathrobes and Bibles, Waves and Words in Katherine Paterson's Jacob I Have Loved," *Children's Literature in Education*, Spring 1986, p. 3.

8 Paterson, *The Invisible Child*, p. 139.

9 Ibid., p. 139.

10 Ibid., p. 100.

11 Ibid., p. 46.

12 Ibid., p. 53.

13 Katherine Paterson, *The Smallest Cow in the World*. New York: HarperCollins, 1986, p. 62.

14 Katherine Paterson, "These Are Questions Recently Asked by Children and Educators in an Internet Interview with Katherine Paterson."

15 "Katherine Paterson," *St. James Guide to Children's Writers*, 5th ed. Farmington Hills, Mich.: St. James Press, 1999. Reproduced in *Biography Resource Center*. Farmington Hills, Mich.: Gale, 2008.

## Chapter 8

1 "Homogeneous." Merriam-Webster Online Dictionary. http://www.merriam-webster.com/dictionary/homogeneous.

2 Paterson, interview.

3 Maura Spiegel, introduction to *The Jungle*, by Upton Sinclair, Barnes&Noble.com. http://search.barnesandnoble.com/The-Jungle/Upton-Sinclair/e/9781593080082#EXC.

4 "Biography." Barnes&Noble.com. http://search.barnesandnoble.com/Uncle-Toms-Cabin/Harriet-Beecher-Stowe/e/9781593081812.

5 Paterson, interview.

6 Katherine Paterson, *Lyddie*. New York: HarperCollins 1991, p. 181.

7 William Howard Tucker, *History of Hartfort, Vermont*; *July 4 1761–April 4, 1889*. Burlington, Vt.: Free Press Association, 1889, p. 308, quoted in Katherine Paterson, *The*

*Invisible Child: On Reading and Writing for Children*. New York: Dutton Children's Books, 2001, pp. 16–17.

8 Katherine Paterson, *Jip*. New York: HarperCollins, 1996, p. 28.

9 Illene Cooper, "Paterson Looks Back," *Booklist*, August 1999, p. 2044.

10 Ibid.

11 Ibid.

12 Curt Anderson, "The Two Countries That Invented the Industrial Revolution." Emachinetool.com. http://www.emachinetool.com/machine_history.cfm.

13 Marie Orlando, "Katherine Paterson, *Bread and Roses, Too* (Brief Review)," *School Library Journal*, September 2006, p. 215.

## Chapter 9

1 Paterson, "These Are Questions Recently Asked by Children and Educators in an Internet Interview with Katherine Paterson."

2 Oleck, "*Bridge to Terabithia* Hits the Big Screen," p. 20.

3 Paterson, interview.

4 Goldberg, *Writing Down the Bones*, pp. 6–7.

5 Paterson, interview.

6 Ibid.

7 Sonya Haskins, "5 Questions: Katherine Paterson," *Writer's Digest*, July 2000, Research Library Core, p. 8.

8 Paterson, *The Invisible Child*, pp. 39–40.

# WORKS BY KATHERINE PATERSON

**1973** *The Sign of the Chrysanthemum*

**1974** *Of Nightingales That Weep*

**1975** *The Master Puppeteer*

**1977** *Bridge to Terabithia*

**1978** *The Great Gilly Hopkins*

**1979** *Angels and Other Strangers: Family Christmas Stories*

**1980** *Jacob Have I Loved*

**1981** *The Crane Wife* by Sumiko Yagawa (as translator); *Gates of Excellence: On Reading and Writing Books for Children*

**1983** *Rebels of the Heavenly Kingdom*

**1985** *Come Sing, Jimmy Jo*

**1986** *Consider the Lilies: Plants of the Bible* (with John Paterson)

**1987** *The Tongue-cut Sparrow* by Momoko Ishii (as translator)

**1988** *Park's Quest*; *The Smallest Cow in the World*

**1989** *The Spying Heart: More Thoughts on Reading and Writing Books for Children*

**1990** *The Tale of the Mandarin Ducks*

**1991** *Lyddie*

**1992** *The King's Equal*

**1994** *Flip-Flop Girl*

**1995** *A Midnight Clear: Stories for the Christmas Season*

**1996** *Jip: His Story*; *The Angel and the Donkey*

**1997** *Marvin's Best Christmas Present Ever*

**1998** *Parzival: The Quest of the Grail Knight* (as reteller)

**1999** *Preacher's Boy*

**2000** *The Wide-awake Princess*

**2001** *The Field of the Dogs*; *Marvin One Too Many*; *The Invisible Child: On Reading and Writing Books for Children*

**2002**  *The Same Stuff as Stars*
**2004**  *Blueberries for the Queen*
**2006**  *Bread and Roses, Too*
**2009**  *The Day of the Pelican*

# POPULAR BOOKS

**BREAD AND ROSES, TOO**

A real-life 1912 strike against a mill owner sends the daughter of a factory worker to Vermont.

**BRIDGE TO TERABITHIA**

Terabithia is a world created by imagination, a place of escape for two best friends. It is a place that nurtures the artist and the dreamer.

**THE GREAT GILLY HOPKINS**

What will a foster child who's been rejected by every foster family that has taken her in do when one unlikely person offers her love? Since that foster child still believes someday she will be rescued by her abandoning mother, the answer is surprising.

**JACOB HAVE I LOVED**

On an isolated island, a girl dreams of escaping and leaving the shadow of the twin she imagines is loved more by both her family and by God.

**JIP**

On a Vermont poor farm, a boy finds himself one step from slavery. Only luck and an unlikely friendship helps him escape.

**LYDDIE**

The toil of the textile mill is an unlikely place for dreams of education and success, but it is in the mill that a farm girl learns to read and aspire.

**THE SIGN OF THE CHRYSANTHEMUM**

In twelfth-century Japan, a young boy named Muna seeks his father, a respected samurai without a name. With only the stories of his now dead mother to go on, he seeks the one with a tattoo of a chrysanthemum.

# POPULAR CHARACTERS

**JESSE AARONS**

An artist who feels lost in his rural town, he finds escape through his imagination and friendship.

**LESLIE BURKE**

Leslie is Jesse's best friend, a girl who beats the boys in races and helps him discover Terabithia. As the new girl from a big city, Leslie and Jesse bond over their outsider status and secret interests.

**LYDDIE**

Lyddie, a hard-working young woman employed at a textile mill in Lowell, Massachusetts, longs to make enough money to reunite her family in Vermont. When that dream fails, she continues to work and save for herself. Money means independence, something few women enjoy in nineteenth-century Vermont. Yet the work in a mill provides more than an income; it provides a friend who teaches her to love books and imagine more for her future.

**SARA LOUISE BRADSHAW**

Nicknamed "Wheeze" by her friends and family, Sara Louise believes she is unloved and unappreciated in *Jacob Have I Loved*. As the pudgier, less attractive counterpart to her twin sister, Sara Louise longs for a life away from her home on a lonely island in the Chesapeake Bay.

# MAJOR AWARDS

**1977** *The Master Puppeteer* wins the National Book Award for Children's Literature.

**1978** *Bridge to Terabithia* wins a Newbery Medal.

**1979** *The Great Gilly Hopkins* is selected as a Newbery Medal Honor Book.

**1981** *Jacob Have I Loved* wins a Newbery Medal.

**1988** *Park's Quest* earns the American Bookseller Pick of the List.

**1991** *The Tale of the Mandarin Ducks* wins the Boston Globe-Horn Book Best Picture Books Selection.

**1994** *Lyddie* is chosen as an International Board of Books for Young People Honor Book (IBBY).

**1999** *Jip* wins the Scott O'Dell Award for Historical Fiction.

# BIBLIOGRAPHY

## Books

Paterson, Katherine. *Gates of Excellence: On Reading and Writing Books for Children*. New York: Dutton Children's Books, 1981.

———. *The Invisible Child: On Reading and Writing Books for Children*. New York: Dutton Children's Books, 2001.

Scott, David Fodor. *Exploring Japan*. New York: Random House, 2008.

## Web Sites

"The Most Frequently Challenged Books of 2007," American Library Association. Available online. URL: http://www.ala.org/ala/ aboutala/offices/oif/bannedbooksweek/challengedbanned/ frequentlychallengedbooks.cfm#miofcb.

"September 11, 2001 Numbers," *New York*. Available online. URL: http:// nymag.com/news/articles/wtc/1year/numbers.htm.

"The Top Ten Challenged Books from 1991," American Library Association. Available online. URL: http://www.ala.org/ala/aboutala/ offices/oif/bannedbooksweek/bbwlists/1991-2007_Top_10.pdf.

# FURTHER READING

Campbell, Joseph. *The Hero with a Thousand Faces*. 1949. Reprint, Novato, Calif.: New World Library, 2008.

Goldberg, Natalie. *Writing Down the Bones: Freeing the Writer Within*. Boston: Shambhala Publications, 1986.

Heinrichs, Ann. *Japan: Enchantment of the World*. New York: Scholastic Books, 2006.

King, Stephen. *On Writing: A Memoir of the Craft*. New York: Pocket Books, 2000.

Lamott, Anne. *Bird by Bird: Some Instructions on Writing and Life*. New York: Pantheon Books, 1994.

# PICTURE CREDITS

page:

10: Buena Vista/Photofest

16: akg-images

23: AP Images

31: ©Topham/The Image Works

34: © yannick luthy/Alamy

46: By Sarah Vogelsang, Katherine Paterson with Nam and Claire from the Kids on the Block-Vermont programs of educational puppetry, www. KidsontheBlockVermont.org.

50: Heiji Uprising of 1159, Momoyama Period (1568–1615) (ink on paper) by Japanese School (16th century) Private Collection/Photo Boltin Picture Library/ The Bridgeman Art Library Nationality/copyright status: Japanese/out of copyright

56: © Dorling Kindersley

63: Times Argus, Jeb Wallace-Brodeur/AP Images

66: Neal Ulevich/AP Images

70: AP Images

78: The Art Archive/School of Oriental & African Studies/ Eileen Tweedy

88: © North Wind Picture Archives/Alamy

100: Buena Vista/Photofest

103: Stephen Shugerman/Getty Images Entertainment/Getty Images

# INDEX

# ABOUT THE CONTRIBUTOR

The author of over four-dozen biographies for young adults, including books on Stephen Hawking, Margaret Mead, and F. Scott Fitzgerald, **JOHN BANKSTON** lives in Newport Beach, California. From the ages of 9 until 16, he lived in Quechee, Vermont, not far from Katherine Paterson's home in Barre. He has worked as an actor, screenwriter, and legal assistant. Currently revising a young-adult novel, *18 to Look Younger*, Bankston does all his first drafts in longhand, on college-ruled notebook paper.